A Book of Hours

MEDITATIONS ON THE TRADITIONAL CHRISTIAN HOURS OF PRAYER

by Patricia Colling Egan

Conciliar Press

Chesterton, Indiana

A Book of Hours
Meditations on the Traditional Christian Hours of Prayer

Published by   Conciliar Press
                  A division of Conciliar Media Ministries
                  P.O. Box 748
                  Chesterton, IN 46304

Printed in the United States of America

ISBN 10: 1-936270-06-4
ISBN 13: 978-1-936270-06-4

      15 14 13 12 11 10   6 5 4 3 2 1

Cover Design by Mark Wainwright, www.symbologycreative.com

Calligraphy by Carla Harris, www.calligraphybycarla.com

For my son,
Benjamin Teilhard Prendergast

TABLE OF CONTENTS

PROLOGUE

Outside my windows a sullen sky, ripped open by the force of waters it can no longer contain, dissolves in torrents. Days have blurred to a sodden greyness that swells leaves, creates pools in hollows, and stills the mind.

These nights I wake to hear gentle clanging. Like a bell buoy bobbing on nocturnal seas the lone wind chime sounds against rushing streams and moanings of wind-tossed limbs. But there will come a morning when, generated in watery woodland darkness, light suffuses the tips of evergreen branches with chartreuse feathers. Born of water and the Spirit . . .

Thrushes, not content with warbling the edges of morning and evening, produce an eccentric soloist at midday who contrives to pierce the silence by fluting at intervals along the afternoon. At the junction of Ledge-wood with Alexander Drive peepers still sing the reprise of their watery joys, and a surplus of screeching rabbits punctuates each night so owls may thrive. Which is simply to say: The full of this year overflows with water and spirit.

A spring so wet conjures up images of ark building, of a world submerged until a dove with a branch in its beak signals renewal; of the Jordan closing over the head of a man from Galilee and the Spirit of God resting on Him in the form of a dove when He rises from the river. "You send forth Your Spirit and renew the face of the earth . . ."

It's June, and whether a Christian inclines to the East or the West, it's Pentecost, season of fullness, of hopeful promise, mirroring and celebrating the descent of the Holy Spirit: genesis of the mysterious gathering we call *ecclesia*. It happened two thousand years ago; it happens *now*. The Holy Spirit descends in our time, creating *ecclesia*—"the Gathering"—renewing us and our earth.

One way to describe those who make up "the Gathering" is prayer. To live in Christ is to pray, is to *become* prayer. Fragments of our lives are thus gathered, offered, and transformed into bread for others, into Eucharist, into the Kingdom of God. Like the turning of a kaleidoscope, prayer draws our bits and pieces into pattern.

To whom do we address our prayer? To the God of the philosophers, a monad of infinite indetermination dwelling so far out in space that He's barely aware of the world He set in motion? Or to a divine Father slowly revealed over time through His Image and His Spirit to be supremely personal, impelled by His love to share life with beings He summoned from nothingness?

Our God is not a gas. Nor is prayer some abstraction that reduces the variability of life to metaphysical gruel. Nevertheless, at times believers treat God as though He were akin to oxygen—invisible, essential, everywhere— and just as elusively impersonal.

How often is "I believe in God" said as though one were doing Him a favor by acknowledging His existence? *Saying* we believe means nothing unless we *do* our belief, unless we encounter the One in whom we believe. *Doing* faith is, at bottom, praying.

Yet even many with genuine faith whose lives are being transformed by it may find prayer difficult or imagine that they don't know how. It is the hope of this book that we, having forgotten a little, may be reminded that we know how to pray, may remove obstacles we place in the way of the Spirit who groans within us.

Westerners know they can pray anywhere, any-time, and often . . . don't. They may confuse prayer with begging for favors or with conversation, then, disappointed on both counts, give up. Easterners may participate in the Divine Liturgy or perform a set order of daily prayers without a sense either of praying or becoming prayer.

Yet if we both, East and West, have within us the mustard seed of faith, of prayer, it can become a mighty tree. Starting out so small as to be nearly invisible, it has the potential to permeate our entire being and through us to leaven, to spread light and savor throughout our world.

To our elder brothers the Jews we owe the custom of praying morning and evening. Remembering God in prayer at the beginning and end of each day acknowledged His dominion over all, keeping Him before the spiritual eyes of the faithful Israelite. At some point, this prayer was extended to other hours throughout the day. The practice of praying the entire Psalter, all 150 psalms, also originated with the Jews. Following their lead, Christians incorporated all the psalms into their formal prayer, eventually achieving the form we find in medieval books of hours.

This *Book of Hours* is divided according to the pre-Vatican II Divine Office of the Western Church. While the underlying conception of the Divine Hours is the same in both East and West, and both are based on chanting the

Psalms, the East has such a superabundance of hymns and other liturgical material that it cannot be contained in one simple format. I beg the reader to forgive liberties I have taken with the letter of the liturgical hours in order to reveal the Spirit behind them and the way they enable us to experience our Tradition.

But aren't books of hours illustrated? Don't they delight the eye with ornate capitals, fanciful images of flowers, fruits, monkeys, and exotic birds embroidering the text? This one, too, will borrow images from creation and Scripture to embellish its thought.

Matins

Orthros

In the beginning, God created the heavens and the earth. Earth was then empty and formless. Darkness covered the abyss; the breath of God swirled above the waters.

GENESIS 1:1–2[1]

At three AM in mid-December windows are still black. It's dark, but this darkness, like that of the wet June night, is the womb of light: of the sun that will urge dead trees into a leafy spring, and of the Son who comes to make an eternal spring of our mortal winters. We are in the time and the season of expectancy and hidden beginnings: Advent.[2]

Here in Maine we are blessed with natural icons of Advent: stark forms of trees stripped of their leaves. If we were distracted by their leafy flutterings in spring, summer, and fall, their leaflessness now invites us to simplicity, to focus on essentials. We perceive underlying structures rather than impressionistic surface images.

The sun, weaker during winter, appears to concentrate what strength it possesses in rising and setting, with colors more dazzling than in the softer seasons. Or perhaps we simply see them better now. If we resist the glitzy pull of frenetic activity, our days are filled with a healthy silence made palpable by lavender skies and the occasional miracle of snow.

In darkness the Eternal Potter shapes the void, breathes life into clay, spinning it on the wheel of time in its long journey toward divinity. In darkness God calls Abraham out of Ur of the Chaldees to a Promised Land.

Advent, the Matins of the year, is a season of singing in the dark, of faith celebrating long centuries of Israel's hopeful waiting and searching, as well as our own seasons of responding to God's call in the night of limited understanding or affliction as we journey to the Kingdom.

The intuition of faithful people throughout the ages has been to pray on rising and going to bed, to bind each day with acknowledgment of the One "in whom we live and move and have our being." Early in Christian history, after the Church adopted the Psalter, she transferred its first morning section from dawn back into the midnight darkness so that no hour would be left unconsecrated.

While a midnight vigil office still remains part of the Eastern tradition, in the West Matins emerged out of *vigiliae* to become a pre-dawn prayer ending before sunrise. What can be confusing today is that although the term *Matins* means morning prayer, in the West it has become the precursor to morning prayer.

In the Orthodox tradition the great morning prayer is still called Matins (*Orthros* in Greek), but the hour called Matins in the West is really a remnant of Vigils, more equivalent to the Eastern midnight service. To further confuse the issue, the great morning prayer of the West is now called Lauds.

Ignoring the tangle of nomenclature, our Matins remains an hour of beginnings chanted while night still prevails. Shadowy forms of monks and nuns tumbling off hard pallets to throw on their habits, then, after a hasty wash, hurrying off to church to sing the darkness toward the light, keep company in the mind with the *tenebrae*[3] of creation, with beginnings.

Among Matins themes like creation and Advent belongs that of Israel, God's chosen people, for Israel is the prehistory of the Christian story, its source. And twined about the roots of Israel's coming to prayer is the idea of blessing. Her early instinct was to "bless" God in return for His gifts, thanking and praising Him. "Bless the Lord, O my soul, and let all that is within me bless His holy name."

From such simple thankfulness, Israel developed her prayer and understanding of God until they culminated in the psalms, religious songs of such beauty and spiritual penetration that they have always formed the basis of the Church's hourly prayer.

As with cosmic Creation, our personal beginning occurs (and recurs) with the Spirit breathing over chaos. We respond to or ignore the still small voice urging us to come forth from disorder and confusion to acknowledge what truly *is*, to relinquish the illusion that self is in charge or that one's own limited point of view determines reality.

Once we say, "It is He who has made us and not we ourselves," we begin to run along the path to freedom, participating in our own creation as a mysterious part of the larger world we are starting to perceive more clearly.

In the Genesis account God shaped the cosmos by parting the waters above from those below and establishing the heavens above the earth. Similarly, we make distinctions in order to shape our personal universe.

Each of us is faced with a fundamental choice: Either life, the world, my existence are meaningful, or they are utterly devoid of meaning. Life has purpose and its evident design serves purposeful ends, or else all is accidental: a hodgepodge of coincidence hurtling toward catastrophe.

Hundreds of years before Christ a psalmist sings of the wonder, beauty, and order of creation, expressing his worship through poetry we have yet to surpass.

> Look! Look up at the rainbow and bless the Author of it.
> How magnificently it spans the heavens,
> That ring of colors traced by the Most High!
> By His order, snow falls; lightning bolts are hurled by His
>   decree.
> They open His storehouse and, like birds, clouds fly out.
> By His power clouds thicken, then shatter into hailstones.
> At the voice of His thunder, earth goes into labor;
> At His glance, mountains tremble.
> By His will, the south wind blows,
> As do hurricanes of the north and cyclones.
> He makes snow drift down like birds coming to roost,
> Settling like a swarm of locusts.
> The eye is filled with wonder before its brilliant whiteness;
> Watching its steady fall stuns the mind.
> He sprinkles frost, too, like salt
> Feather-stitching the frozen earth.

Cold blasts of northern wind glaze the waters,
Icing the still pond with a coat of mail.
When heat consumes mountains and singes plains,
Stripping them of their green like a fire,
Rain clouds supply the remedy:
Their drops restore joy to the land after the scorching
    heat.
His wisdom subdues the sea, planting islands on it.
Mariners relate the dangers of the sea;
Their tales astonish us with surprising life forms
And strange monsters of the deep.
Thanks to God, each has its message to bear,
Fulfilling the plan according to His word.
Why do we go on and on like this?
Because He is all in all!
Let us praise Him more, unfathomable as He is,
For He surpasses all His works, great as they are. . . .
He remains even more full of mystery than our paltry
    glimpses
Of His work suggest. For He created all of it,
Rewarding with wisdom those who worship Him.
(ECCLESIASTICUS 43:11–33)

We can avoid acknowledging the One who is the source of meaning, of creation, of our lives, through a kind of intellectual sleight-of-hand. We can live as though there are pockets of meaning, yet maintain that the whole has none. In this way we postpone the implications of our creaturehood, pretending that *we* are God and making up the "rules" as we go along. This approach is not without consequences. For, if the whole is meaningless, there can be no "pockets of meaning." Depression and suicide make perfect sense in such a senseless universe.

Once we understand that we dwell in an intelligible cosmos, that the Creator has purpose, our response is to seek both the meaning of our own existence and the One who bestows and sustains it. And when we embark on such a search, we begin to pray. Like the void, our prayer is formless and empty but, although "darkness covers the abyss," "the breath of God is swirling above the waters."

In the creation story God divides light from darkness on the fourth day. Like Him, in whose image we are created, we too must divide light from darkness all the days of our life. The search for what is, for the truth of things, is a kind of rudimentary prayer. We come to know and love the Creator when we appreciate and understand what He has made.

But is there nothing to prayer in this dark, formless place, this time before sunrise, beyond seeking truth? Is there no other way? There is. Faced with the presence of the One who creates us, who is beyond our ability to comprehend, we may be impelled to pray the prayer of prostration.

In such cases it relieves us to acknowledge the

distance between creature and Creator by bowing to the ground. We stretch full length on the earth, in effect saying, "I am from nothing and, without You, am nothing. Thank You for the life You have given me. Forgive me, for 'against You only have I sinned.'" If we seek Him, we shall find Him, and if we knock, He will surely open the door.

St. Theophan the Recluse tells us that prayer is "standing with our mind in our heart before God."[4] No matter what we are doing or what form our prayer takes, this is the essence of it. We draw our mind, afflicted as it so often is with distractions (like mosquitoes or gnats, St. Theophan says), down into the depths of our heart, lifting our whole being to God, in whose presence we acknowledge ourselves to be.

Everything else we do in prayer is an elaboration of St. Theophan's definition. Without the effort to make ourselves aware that we live our lives in the sight of God, life is ultimately meaningless.

Outside the consciousness of His loving presence, words directed to God are empty. So, in addition to seeking His face and praying the prayer of prostration, we make an effort to collect ourselves before praying, taking a step back from the clamor of earthly existence into the presence of the One who sustains it all for His purposes.

To the Jews we not only owe the custom of praying at

designated intervals, but from them we have also inherited the psalms. Psalm 1 is about us, describing the seeker of truth, one who tries to separate light from darkness. Later, Christians viewed it as describing Christ, since He alone fulfills the ideal of the just man.

> Happy indeed is the man
> Who follows not the counsel of the impious;
> Who neither lingers in the company
> Of those who have lost their way,
> Nor sits down where the scornful gather,
> But whose delight is in the law of the Lord
> And who ponders His law day and night.
> He is like a tree planted near flowing waters,
> Ready to yield fruit in due season,
> And whose leaves never wither.
> All that he does shall prosper.
> Not so are the impious, not so!
> For they, like winnowed chaff,
> Shall be swept away by the wind.
> When the impious are judged, they shall not
> Rise up to plead their cause,
> Nor will those who have strayed
> Find themselves among the holy.
> For the Lord knows the way of the holy,
> But the way of the wicked loses itself.

Praying the psalm illumines us. We begin to see by its light until that light is within us. And we join generation on generation of Jews and Christians before us praying the same psalm in other times and other places, finding our way through darknesses in their company.

Here at the roots of prayer three things are essential. First we must make that division of interior light from darkness: rejecting the shadows of meaninglessness and embracing the light, the One who creates. "Thou shalt love the Lord thy God with the love of thy whole heart, and thy whole soul and thy whole mind and thy whole strength."

Prayer inevitably follows, for genuine acknowledgment of God alters our universe. No longer imagining ourselves at its center, we are impelled to worship the One who is. Our being falls down in humility before Him. Gratitude wells up in us, awe and penitence. We hear the words of John the Baptist: "Repent, the Kingdom of Heaven is at hand."

The Greek noun we translate as "repentance" is *metanoia*. It means profound change of heart: turning from darkness to light, from evil to good, from the created to the Creator. It reverses the sin of Adam, which was to turn from the Creator to the created. Adam separated himself from God, losing the ability to see creation from God's perspective by preferring his own.

The second essential is to embrace the reality of our

own death. We will die to this life. From physical death there is no escape. For inhabitants of a meaningless universe death is the final absurdity, the mere thought of which sends them scampering to burrow among vanities and addictions. Those undergoing *metanoia*, already beginning to experience the life of the Kingdom of God, have no fear of physical death, but keep it before their eyes as a way to put everything temporal in perspective.

Medieval dramatists used death as a magnifying glass in their morality plays. By situating Everyman on his deathbed they applied the lens of impending mortality to every facet of his life.

Viewed in the shadow of death, life becomes more vivid. Things align themselves in relation to their end, and Everyman is forced to recognize that he must say goodbye to wealth, health, youth, acknowledging as vanity most of the illusions he has pursued. These will not keep him company on his journey beyond the grave.

> O Lord, warn me of my end and how brief are the days
>> allotted to me;
> Teach me to know how fleeting I am!
> Behold, You have measured a short span of days for me:
> Nothing but a breath, every man who stands tall;
> Nothing but a shadow, the one who struts about the
>> world;

Nothing but a breath, the riches he heaps up
Without knowing who will enjoy them.
(PSALM 39:4–6)

Is *Everyman* meant to leave its audience depressed, regretting wasted opportunities? No. The hope is rather that presenting a deathbed perspective will enhance life, inspiring individuals to pursue what endures, to build on rock. A healthy awareness of our own death concentrates us: We move toward the defining moment of our earthly sojourn, weighting the goods of this life as they relate to what lies beyond it.

When we embrace the certainty and finality of our own death, each moment of earthly life intensifies. Knowing that time is finite only increases its preciousness. We begin to comprehend our lives as developing sequentially through seasons, the alternation of night and day, in places.

One sunrise or one sunset is not enough, but they must be repeated every day. Neither can one winter or one spring accomplish their work in us. In, through, and behind the shifting scenery of our days Someone continually calls us, Someone we are incapable of seeing or apprehending without help.

The third essential is gratitude: a deep, abiding

thankfulness for life, for each day and every moment in it. Psalm 103, said or sung at every Orthodox Matins service, expresses gratitude, and with it our praise and adoration. Praying it joins us to the chorus of Jewish and Christian voices who also prayed it down the centuries, allowing the Spirit who inspired the psalmist to inform us.

Bless the Lord, O my soul;
And all that is within me, bless His holy name!
Bless the Lord, O my soul,
And forget not all His benefits.
It's He who forgives all your sins,
Healing all your infirmities;
Who redeems your life from the grave,
Crowning you with His love and tenderness;
Who fills your mouth with good things
To restore your youth like the eagle's plumage.
The Lord works justice and righteousness
For all who are oppressed.
He made his ways known to Moses,
His deeds to the children of Israel.
The Lord is merciful and gracious,
Slow to anger and abounding in mercy.
His wrath has an end; nor will He
Remember our offenses forever.
He neither treats us as our sins deserve
Nor renders to us in the measure of our wrongdoing.
High as the heavens are above the earth,

So strong is His love for those who fear Him.
Far as East is from West,
So far has He removed our sins from us.
As a father's tenderness for His children,
So is the Lord's compassion for those who fear Him;
For He knows of what we are made;
He remembers that we are dust.
As for man, his days are like grass;
Like a flower of the field he blooms;
The hot wind passes over and it is gone,
Forgotten by the very place where it grew.
But the love of the Lord lasts forever
For those who reverence Him,
And His holiness reaches children's children
When they keep His covenant,
Remembering to fulfill His will.
The Lord has fixed His throne in the heavens,
His dominion over all.
Bless the Lord, you, His angels,
Mighty in power, who carry out His wishes,
Attentive to the sound of His voice.
Bless the Lord, all you His hosts,
His servants who do His will.
Bless the Lord, all His works,
In every corner of His dominion.

Matins, like beginning, never ends. We may move on to Lauds, but Matins, once set in motion, reverberates throughout our lives, awakening us to the touch of our

Creator as He fashions us through time. Let us seek His face in the certainty that if we seek, if we follow the star, like the Magi of old we shall find.

In this book of hours, a miniature accompanies Matins, its frame of angels, shepherds, sheep, and kings interspersed with green holly leaves and red berries. A single star shines from the center of the upper border:

Snow is falling in the black silence outside his window as an elderly Russian gentleman bends intently over the open top drawer of his desk. His study is dark, maps carpeting its walls dimly illumined by a single lamp on his desk. The shape of a globe, barely visible, and piles of other maps littering every surface betray his profession. Yet, ignoring the charts of the world he loves to study, the white-haired geographer seems lost in contemplation of the lamp-lit drawer before him.

I owe this image to Galina Tregubov, who related to me an incident in her Soviet childhood. Her grandfather, the geographer, often worked at home in a study filled with maps. He kept the top drawer of his desk locked, never allowing anyone near it, never disclosing what he kept there. From time to time Galina would observe him from a distance, utterly fascinated by whatever that drawer contained. To penetrate the mystery of the drawer became the little girl's obsession.

One day, while it was open, her grandfather suffered a stroke. While everyone else was distracted by the event, the unnoticed child tiptoed to the drawer to view its mysterious secret: an icon and a prayer book.

Fearful of consequences to his children and grandchildren, Galina's grandfather had not instructed them in the faith. Yet his silent prayer functioned as a beacon against the darkness of the atheism raging outside his windows, its light remaining in her memory to this day.

> The heavens declare the glory of God,
> The vault of heaven betrays His handiwork;
> Day after day the tale is told
> And night after night this revelation is whispered.
> No story is heard, nor any language,
> No audible voice,
> But their silent influence penetrates every land
> Until their message reaches the ends of the earth.
> God made the sky a pavilion for the sun,

Which, like a bridegroom coming from his bed,
Rejoices the way a champion runner does,
Seeing his course before him.
It has its rising at the edge of the heavens
And its course extends to the other side.
From its burning heat none can escape.
The law of the Lord is perfect, a tonic for the soul;
The testimony of the Lord is truthful,
Wisdom for the simple.
How just are the precepts of the Lord,
Gladdening the heart!
The command of the Lord is clear,
Giving light to the eyes.
How holy the fear of the Lord, binding forever.
The decrees of the Lord are truthful
And all of them, just.
They are more to be desired than gold,
And sweeter they are than honey
Dripping from the comb.
(PSALM 19:1–10)

Out of the Matins darkness light will come; from its womb the Child will be born.

LAUDS

PRAISES

In times past, God spoke in fragmentary and varied ways to our fathers through the prophets. In this final age, He expresses Himself through His Son, whom He has made heir of all things and through whom He created the universe. Reflected radiance of the Father's splendor and full expression of His being, He sustains all in the power of His Word. HEBREWS 1:1–3

S unrise is gradual where I live. Banners of apricot or rose, more or less vivid, ribbon-like or applied in bold swathes, usually precede the glowing orb, which must climb above the trees to be noticed. The coming of light here is a gentle affair of golden fingers probing the darkness, combing leaves with tentative brightness or falling in sunny puddles here and there.

In the Middle East it's more sudden. Our miniature for Lauds is H. V. Morton's description of the sun rising at Gaza as his train travels from Egypt to Jerusalem.

And now, as we went onward, I saw a gathering tumult in the east. A white, palpitating light was filling the sky. It was like something approaching at great speed, a mighty army with its chariots and its horsemen. Swords of light thrust their way upward, catching stray clouds and turning them to banners of pink and gold. Then, like an orange flung into the air, the sun leapt up, fully armed, into the sky; it was warm and the dead earth was instantly, vividly, and rather violently, alive.[5]

Lauds is the hour when light dawns. No longer do we grope in the dark for the lineaments of the face of God. We have *seen* them in the countenance of Jesus, the carpenter from Nazareth. Just as the sudden light of the sun transforms the lifeless, monochromatic landscape of pre-dawn Palestine, the Son of God transfigures our personal landscapes.

With a self-emptying beyond our comprehension, the Creator penetrates His world to live and die as a human being. In so doing, He changes the water of earthly existence into the wine of eternal life through the power of the Holy Spirit unleashed by His presence among us.

> Blessed be the name of the Lord
> From this time forth and forevermore!
> From the rising of the sun to its setting
> The name of the Lord is to be praised!
> (PSALM 113:2–3)

In the beginning the Father created water through His Word, and His Spirit hovered above it. With the coming of Christ and His baptism there is a new creation. He through whom all was made plunges into the waters beneath the surface of the earth, imparting His Spirit to them and from them to the world through which they flow, vivifying and refreshing the entire cosmos.

Water, the basic matter of the first creation, also establishes the second. When the Eastern Church celebrates Christ's baptism on Epiphany, her liturgy swirls, rushes, sparkles, and swells with pellucid imagery. The crystalline sound and movement of living water rushes over us, rinsing us with a flood of light-filled poetry to dramatize the cosmic significance of the baptism of Christ and thus, of our own.

In his book, *The Spirit of Early Christian Thought*, Robert Louis Wilken excerpts Tertullian's treatise on baptism, written about the year AD 200:

> Water, he [Tertullian] says, was the first element "to produce things that would live." It is not surprising that water, ordinary water, used in baptism "already knows how to give life." Through the presence of the Holy Spirit water that was precious in itself "took on the ability to make holy." So much is water part of God's way of relating to human beings, he [Tertullian] writes, that "Christ was never without water. He himself was baptized with water; when invited to a marriage he inaugurates the exercise of his power with water; when talking he invites the thirsty to partake of his own everlasting water; when teaching about charity he approves among the works of love the offering of a cup of water to a neighbor; he refreshes his strength at a well-side; he walks on water; he crosses it at will; he uses water to do an act of service to his disciples. This witness to baptism continues right up to the passion. When he is handed over to the cross, water plays a part (witness Pilate's hands); and when he is pierced, water gushes out from his side.[6]

What does water have to do with prayer or Lauds? Through the mystery of His Incarnation Christ immerses Himself in human nature; at His baptism He is seen penetrating the earth itself, going below its surface into the depths of the river, into water, the basic material of creation.[7] (Scientists actually confirm ancient intuition when they acknowledge that we are mostly water.) Now the entire cosmos is bathed in the luminescence of Christ, so that one aspect of our prayer must be consciousness of this altered milieu.

Because God, through His Word, has taken on flesh and, through His flesh, the cosmos, we who have died with Him in baptism rise from the waters endowed with a capacity for divine life in Him. Water, our basic element, has itself been "soaked" in Christ and, through it, so have we. Our response is Lauds, praise, prayer . . .

Not only have we been shown God's "face," we know from the revelation at Christ's baptism that God is triune. God is the Father through whose Word we are created and recreated and whose Spirit labors within us, "fulfilling all things," a divine embrace of personality rather than a distant, solitary divinity.

In the creation story, Adam's rejection of his true position as a creature, his failure to recognize the abyss separating his nature from God's, led him to fashion God in his own image. Adam believed the serpent's words to Eve which implied that God was merely being a petty tyrant in forbidding the fruit—that He was just preventing Adam from enjoying the fullness of existence and knowledge.

In so doing, Adam imagined that the only thing between him and divinity was the forbidden fruit: the fruit of the tree of the knowledge of good and evil. His was the archetypal arrogance that infects each of us when we reject God and choose to sin. Sin ruptures the intimacy we are meant to enjoy with God, and its reverberations are cosmic.

Adam succeeded in his attempt at usurping the divine prerogative. He became creator—and, in a sense, he created out of nothingness. He created a world out of the nothingness of his sin, and all of his descendants are born into his sinful world. The first secularist, without destroying its beauty, distorted God's creation by seeing it and himself independently of God, thus generating the ugly brood of evil and sin in which we are all immersed from birth.[8]

To heal that rupture, those distortions, and to achieve the fulfillment of our nature, we need help from outside ourselves as well as from within our humanness. We need God in our flesh, just what we have been given but could never have envisioned. Christ's life, so humanly true and full, so united to the Father, restores the harmony, the *shalom*, of the cosmos.

He is "the Way, the Truth, and the Life" (John 14:6) we must follow, seek, and live if we are to fulfill in ourselves and our time the healing and restoration He accomplished in His own. He is the new Adam reversing His predecessor's pseudo-creation, restoring to the world its capacity for God.

We now know with infinitely more precision the One to whom our prayer is directed, for we have been shown the image of the Father in human flesh. St. John says, "That which was from the beginning, which we have heard, which we have seen with our eyes, which we looked upon and have touched with our hands, concerning the word of life—that life was made manifest. We have seen it, and we testify to it and proclaim to you the eternal life which was with the Father and was shown to us" (1 John 1–2).

For those who have plunged with Christ into baptismal water, the change is radical, an alteration in our being far beyond what intellectual acknowledgment or even imitation could produce. We may choose not to actualize it in our lives, but we have been incorporated into Christ's death by baptism and into His life through the anointing with oil and the gift of the Holy Spirit. We are able to participate in "christening" the cosmos and returning it (at least the part we touch), healed by love, to the Father. Lauds alters everything.

"But," says the modern whom shadows still afflict, "*we* have neither seen nor heard Him. *We* have never touched Him with our hands." Lauds insists we have. Like the blood and water issuing from the side of Christ crucified, a river of Holy Tradition gushes from His body in time—the body of those born anew into his life: *Ecclesia*, the Gathering, the Church.

Despite her fumbling human ways the Church has preserved the image of Christ. We hear His voice in the Gospels; we see His face in icons lovingly painted as well as in the countenances of the saints; we touch Him when we serve His "little ones" and we taste Him in union with all the faithful when we receive His body and blood in the Holy Eucharist.

> O sing to the Lord a new song; sing to the Lord all the
>   earth!
> Sing to the Lord, bless His name; tell of His salvation from
>   day to day.
> Declare His glory among the nations,
> His marvelous works among all the peoples!
>
> * * * * *
>
> Let the heavens be glad and let the earth rejoice;

Let the sea roar and all that fills it;
Let the field exult and everything in it!
Then shall all the trees of the forest sing for joy before the
    Lord,
For He comes, He comes to judge the earth.
He will judge the world by holiness
And the peoples in His faithfulness.
(FROM PSALM 96)

How does an encounter with Christ come about? Within the framework of each day He comes to meet all who seek the Way, the Truth, and the Life. He is there in every season, every event, accessible to all who seek, whether or not they pronounce His name. Faith, trusting in the still, small voice, as did Abraham, leads us out of (and into) each hour to Him.

Like Moses, we may experience moments when appearances give way, moments of transfiguration when what we see is on fire with the presence of "I AM" and we know ourselves to be in a holy place. At other times, we may seem to wander in the wilderness, God's presence no more than an incomprehensible, beckoning cloud. In darkness, we may perceive only a pillar of fire, a hint of the light, warmth, and truth we are to follow. The prayer of faith keeps her eyes on both.

By faith His contemporaries recognized Christ in the

man walking at their side toward Emmaus, and it is by faith that we penetrate appearances to recognize Him in Holy Scripture, in the Eucharist, in holy men and women vivified by His life. Should our own faith seem deficient, we can pray as did the father of the possessed boy in the Gospel: "Lord, I believe; help my unbelief" (Mark 9:24).

Jesus cried out and said, "Whoever believes in Me, believes not in Me but in Him who sent Me. And whoever sees Me sees Him who sent Me" (John 12:44–45). Symbolic of our joyous response to the Son of God's rising in our midst, Lauds is a shout of praise and gratitude. No longer greyed by the shadow of permanent death, we are free to live in Technicolor, to dwell in the presence of God revealed in His Son.

Like the vigorous Middle Eastern sun catapulting into the heavens, Christ illumines our interior universe, warming our days with His love, chasing shadows of uncertainty and fear. He demonstrates that the face of our awesome, all-powerful God is that of a loving Father running to meet us once we turn from our prodigal squandering ways among the pigs.

> Shout with joy to the Lord, all the earth!
> Serve the Lord with gladness;
> Come before Him singing for joy!
> Know that He, the Lord, is God.

He made us; we belong to Him.
We are His people, the sheep of His flock.
Enter His gates with thanksgiving
And His courts, with praise!
Give thanks to Him, bless His name!
For the Lord is good;
His steadfast love endures forever
And His faithfulness to all generations.
(PSALM 100)

"All very well and good," you say. "But how do we recognize Him? Plenty of people claim to speak for Christ, some with conflicting messages." In the words of a contemporary iconographer, Emilie Van Taack:

If it is truly He, . . . even if we have never heard Him spoken of before, His Image is inscribed in the depths of our nature, *we recognize Him and we recognize ourselves in Him.* We are all His sheep: *The sheep follow Him (the Good Shepherd) because they know His voice.* "I know My sheep and they know Me as the Father knows Me and I know the Father . . ." If our quest is sincere, we will certainly find Him. But one must *actively* seek. "Seek and you shall find," He promised.[9]

Part of seeking is studying the Scriptures prayerfully. The Gospels were left us by saints who had encountered Christ themselves or knew others who had. Inspired by the Holy Spirit, they left us not a history, not a biography, but a portrait.

God, by becoming one of us, entrusted Himself to His creatures with all their limitations and flaws. In Gospel accounts of Christ such flaws are evident: imperfect memory, conflicting details. Yet these human attempts at imaging Him for future generations breathe. If we approach them with humility and a desire to find Christ, the Holy Spirit who inspires both the seeker and Holy Scripture will reveal Him to us.

Nor do we have to make this journey alone. In fact it can be dangerous to do so. For our ability to discern develops, as does our prayer, over the whole course of our transfiguration, our *theosis*.[10] "Blessed are those whose hearts have been purified. They shall see God" (Matthew 5:8). In the beginning, when we first step into the Way, we need the company of those who have gone before us, who have achieved the purity of heart to which we aspire.

A favorite image of *ecclesia* is the ark. Transporting a remnant of humanity and creation, it sails over turbulent waters to renewed life, indicated by the dove with the olive branch in its mouth. Those fortunate enough to be on board will find among their companions many whose wisdom and holiness can enlighten and support them in their seeking. But the indispensable guide is God's Holy

Spirit. To the degree that He dwells in us we recognize Him in others, in Holy Scripture, in the breaking of bread. Knowing Christ, learning Him, is the way we grow in the Holy Spirit, become His truth, live His life.

"Be still and know that I am God" (Psalm 46:10). If we listen to God's voice, not only will we recognize His presence, at times we will recognize His absence. We will question the wolf in sheep's clothing, the deceiver who poses as Christian, the false presented as true.

"Ask and you shall receive" (Matthew 7:7). We only need to ask for the Discerner:

> Heavenly King, Comforter, Spirit of Truth,
> who are everywhere present fulfilling all things,
> Treasury of blessing and Giver of life, come and
> abide in us. Cleanse us from every stain and heal us,
> O Good One.

Orthodox priests pray this prayer to the Holy Spirit before every liturgical action, and the faithful are encouraged to pray it often, especially as we begin an undertaking.

God is incomprehensible—but not unknowable. He can be known to some extent through the works of His hands, but it is in Christ, the fullness of the revelation of the Father, that we are able to know Him through the medium of our own nature.

We know Christ through our human nature, yet it is not by imposing that nature on Him, but rather by allowing His to inform ours. This happens through exposure to Christ in the Gospels and reflections on Him in the other writings of the New Testament. The Church, through her liturgy, provides us with foundational readings from Scripture, but we must still refine our knowledge of Christ by supplementing them with our own. Once we have truly tasted Christ, our appetite to know Him increases, and we cannot be satisfied with occasional or partial glimpses of Him mediated by others.

Checking our scriptural explorations and the "mathematics" of our efforts to live Christ against encounters with Him in the Divine Liturgy prevents excessive wandering in wildernesses of our own construction. If we do this, we'll find that the peace-loving, serene Master is also the one who overturned tables of money-changers in the Temple and, brandishing a whip, drove sheep and oxen out with their sellers.

His uncompromising, "If your right eye causes you to sin, tear it out and throw it away" (Matthew 5:29), issues from the tender heart that rescues a trembling woman caught in adultery from her hypocritical accusers. "Has no one accused you?"

She said, "No one, Lord."

"Neither will I condemn you. Go, and from now on, sin no more" (John 8:3–11).

A life spent in the hill country of Galilee—learning the trade of a carpenter, encountering caravans from Damascus or traders from Tyre and Sidon with all their news and wares from the rest of the Mediterranean world, among fishermen by the lovely Sea of Galilee bustling with commerce—is the seminary for a teacher who confounded His hearers in the Temple with His wisdom and authority. "The Jews therefore marveled, saying, 'How is it that this man has learning when He has never studied?'" (John 7:15). "And when Jesus finished these sayings, the crowds were astonished at His teaching, for He was teaching them as one who had authority, not as their scribes" (Matthew 7:28–29).

His harsh words for unfaithful scribes and Pharisees, "Woe to you, scribes and Pharisees, hypocrites! For you are like white-washed tombs which outwardly appear beautiful but within are full of dead men's bones and rottenness" (Matthew 23:27), are followed by His anguish for their city:

"O Jerusalem, Jerusalem, city that kills the prophets and stones those who are sent to it! How often would I have gathered your children together as a hen gathers her chickens under her wings, and you would not!"   (MATTHEW 23:37)

"I have come that you may have life and have it more abundantly" (John 10:10). He Himself is both life and the way to it. Study of that life is seeking Him, and can also be prayer.

Sometimes we need liberation from our times as much as from our ignorance. Again the ark comes to our rescue. Among its two hundred centuries of saints we find holy fathers of the Church whose wisdom and intelligence remain fresh despite the passage of time.

Such marvels of faithful insight as those left us by Syriac fathers like St. Ephraim and St. Isaac or the profound holiness of St. Irenaeus, St. Basil, or St. Gregory of Nyssa will reward their disciples with unsurpassed treasures of mind and spirit. Hear the voice of St. Isaac of Nineveh, still fresh after fourteen hundred years:

> This life has been given you for *metanoia*. Do not waste it in vain pursuits.
>
> Speech is the organ of this present world. Silence is a mystery of the world to come.
>
> Be at peace with your own soul; then heaven and earth will be at peace with you. Enter eagerly into the treasure house that is within you, and you will see the things that are in heaven; for there is but one single

entry to them both. The ladder that leads to the kingdom is hidden in your soul. Flee from sin, dive into
yourself, and in your soul you will discover the stairs
by which to ascend.[11]

Holy Mother Church garners the harvest of *all* her
centuries. Not for her the concept of a "progress" that
obliterates the past as it chugs into the future, arrogantly
certain that the latest idea is necessarily better than what
preceded it. The value of our own strivings and seekings,
our own discoveries, rests solidly on the specific accomplishments of those who strove and sought before us. The
shout of joy that is Lauds is for the whole Christ, extend-
ing and incarnating through every century.

How did the Master define prayer? When His disciples asked Him to teach them to pray, He did not deliver
a discourse, He simply prayed:

Our Father, who art in heaven,
Hallowed be thy name.
Thy Kingdom come,
Thy will be done on earth as it is in heaven.
Give us this day our daily bread
And forgive us our debts as we forgive our debtors.
And lead us not into temptation
But deliver us from evil.
(MATTHEW 6:9–13)

Just by repeating these words "standing with our mind in our heart before God," we are shaped into prayer. Facing the Father, we acknowledge that He is other, that He is not of this world but of a holiness we cannot comprehend, only reverence. We ask that His realm come among us so that His will may be accomplished here as well as where He dwells. We acknowledge our dependence on Him for our daily needs, begging forgiveness. Indebted to Him, we are unable to pay unless we have the kind of heart that forgives others.

Some interpret the "debtor passage" as though God withholds His love and forgiveness to punish us because we withhold ours from others. But we have only one heart. If it is closed to our fellows, it is also closed to God. We, not God, obstruct His forgiveness.

We ask not to be led into temptation. The Greek which we translate as "not to be led into" seems rather to mean "not to be handed over to," for we will certainly be tried by temptation in this world.

The final petition is for deliverance, not simply from evil, but from the evil one. (Again we are indebted to the Greek. *Poniros* can be translated as "evil," but in certain contexts it refers to Satan.) Evil, like temptation, is part of our wounded world, and overcoming it, an important ingredient in our transformation. This last request is not for deliverance from suffering or misfortune but for the kind of discernment capable of unmasking the deceiver. Those who wish to progress in prayer will learn of the Master and devoutly pray His prayer.

From Matins the theme of beginning and seeking, like a thread weaving its way through the fabric of our lives, remains with us long after darkness has given way to light. What thread lingers after Lauds?

Praise, *laus perennis*, perennial praise like filaments of joyful music, penetrates the entire fabric. For the time of seeking the face of God in the darkness is past. He has taken flesh like ours so that it might reveal Him in our own nature, a medium we can understand.

Praise and gratitude well up in us for every one of God's gifts, but when we realize that they are all in and through Christ, that He is the ultimate gift, the others are more truly experienced. As we learn to see Him, as the interpenetration of His image with our own develops, however grim or difficult the "water" of our earthly existence, we taste it as wine.

Sometimes our response is silently to lift our hearts; sometimes we break into song like the psalmist, or like the author of the Akathist prayer, "Glory to God for All

Things," found in 1940 among the effects of Father Gregory Petrov, who died imprisoned in a Russian camp.[12] Here is a small piece of it, the Twefth Ikos:

> What sort of praise can I give You? I have never heard the song of the cherubim, a joy reserved for the spirits above. But I know the praises that nature sings to You.
>
> In winter I have beheld how silently in the moonlight the whole earth, clad in its white mantle of snow, sparkling like diamonds, offers You prayer.
>
> I have seen how the rising sun rejoices in You, how the song of the birds is a chorus of praise to You.
>
> I have heard the mysterious mutterings of forests about You, of winds singing Your praise as they stir the waters.
>
> I have understood how choirs of stars proclaim Your glory as they move perpetually in the depths of infinite space.
>
> What is my poor worship? All nature obeys You; I do not. Yet while I live I see Your love, I long to thank You, pray to You, and call upon Your name.
>
> Glory to You, who give us light.
>
> Glory to You, who love us with love so deep, divine, and infinite.
>
> Glory to You, who bless us with light, and with the host of angels and saints.
>
> Glory to You, Father all-holy, who promise us a share in Your kingdom.

Glory to You, Holy Spirit, life-giving sun of the world
    to come.
Glory to You for all things, holy and most merciful
    Trinity.
Glory to You, O God, from age to age.

To the *Shema Y'israel*, "Hear, O Israel, the Lord is our God, the only God,"[13] is now added the *Eidomen to Fos*, "We have *seen* the Light," which Orthodox Christians sing after receiving Holy Communion. No longer is the Word revealed only to our ears, but our eyes may encounter Him as well. Which brings us to the subject of icons, so intimately connected with the Incarnation of the Word.

The Greek word *eikon* means image, particularly in the sense of a derived likeness, a manifestation. The Word, the full expression of the Father, is His *eikon*, an image so complete that it too is a person.

> Philip said to Him, "Lord, show us the Father, and it is enough for us."
>
> Jesus said to him, "Have I been so long with you, Philip, and you still do not know Me? Whoever has seen Me has seen the Father." (JOHN 14:8–9)

All iconography descends from this desire to see the face of God. Now that He has shown us His countenance in Christ it's possible to attempt a likeness of it for those who, down the centuries, also desire to see and reverence Him.

But what does an icon have to do with prayer? When we pray, a human personality meets divine personality. Persons are not revealed, nor do they communicate, exclusively through words. The genuine icon reveals the essence of the person or mystery depicted. It allows an encounter between our being and the being presented in the icon.

In the words of Henri Nouwen: "[Icons] are created for the sole purpose of offering access, through the gate of the visible, to the mystery of the invisible. Icons are painted to lead us into the inner room of prayer and bring us close to the heart of God."[14]

> Icons . . . as St. Dionysius the Areopagite says, are "visible images of mysterious and supernatural visions." An icon is therefore always either more than itself in becoming for us an image of a heavenly vision, or less than itself in failing to open our consciousness to the world beyond our senses—then it is merely a board with some paint on it.[15]

Westerners, afflicted by abstraction and theory or overstimulated by bombardment of their senses, need not remain passive in the face of the onslaught. Like their Eastern brethren, they too may enter the Kingdom of God through the holy doors of the icon.

There perspective is inverted. What we see in the icon does not recede from us, as though our point of view were the one determining the reality depicted—objects gaining or diminishing in size and importance in proportion to their distance from us. Instead, we are invited to enter a reality greater than we are, one independent of us. "Inverted perspective" corrects our vision, orders our cosmos by transporting us from the center to a point of view capable of apprehending the true center and our relation to Him.

Just as cosmos orders chaos, the icon brings order and peace to our senses. Standing reverently before an icon, allowing it to inform us, we respond to its gaze. We slip into wordless prayer, allowing the Kingdom of God to penetrate beneath the shallow surface of our lives.

In what frame of mind do we stand before the icon? We stand with our mind in our heart, at the point where our insignificance before God and the glory bestowed on us through the Incarnation intersect.

> O Lord, what is man that You take notice of him
> Or the son of man that You keep him in mind?

Man is like the wind; his days pass like a shadow.
(Psalm 144:3–4)

This is a partial reprise of the question asked in Psalm 8. It's as though the answer given in that psalm didn't quite satisfy:

When I look at Your heavens, the work of Your fingers,
The moon and the stars which You have set in place,
What is man that You are mindful of him,
And the son of man that You care for him?
You have made him a little less than the angels
And crowned him with glory and honor.
You have given him dominion over the works of Your
    hands;
You have put all things under his feet:
All sheep and oxen, and also the beasts of the field,
The birds of the heavens, the fish of the sea
That pass through the pathways of the seas.
O Lord, our Lord, how majestic is Your name in all
    the earth!
(Psalm 8:3–9)

The full answer to the psalmist's question comes only in Christ, the icon of the Father. Christ is why God regards us. He is the "why" of creation as well as the "how": "All things came into being through Him and without Him nothing that has been made was made" (John 1:3).

Is there a prayer position for Lauds? Yes. We now pray standing in the presence of God. No longer merely servants, we have been invited into God's family as adopted children. The nature debased by Adam has been recapitulated in Christ; our horizons extend endlessly, now not even limited by death. So we stand erect, joyful and conscious of the dignity bestowed on us.

Over the course of this chapter our miniature has altered.

The sun vaulting into the morning sky now fills the picture, radiating so much light that it spills into the border as a dazzling series of light rays: white, golden, pale peach with a tinge of coral. At the center of the light is a face. The source of all this abundant, pressed down, spilling over light is the sixth-century icon of Christ Pantokrator from the ancient monastery at Sinai.[16]

"Be still and know that I am God."

PRIME

FIRST HOUR

For just as the body is one and has many members, and all the members of the body, though many, are one body, so it is with Christ. For in one Spirit we were all baptized into one body—Jews or Greeks, slaves or free—all were made to drink of one Spirit.

1 CORINTHIANS 12:13

ale morning light steals over an equally pale palette of grey and taupe tree trunks supporting the muted greens of winter-weary conifers. Here and there, like blobs of celestial paint, crocuses converse in purple and lilac about the somber earth.

A smattering of scylla erupts near a balsam fir on an island of brown mulch like shards of sapphire splashed from a Greek harbor. Both day and year are new, unaware

of the fullness to which they are summoned but capable of colorful spurts and splotches like daffodils poking through lifeless earth, apple blossoms startling the sky, or a saint here and there shaking up an era.

Prime (six AM) shares with spring and early morning both newness and the sort of clarity emphasized by contrast. We can't absorb the warmth and brilliance of sun all at once; it will have to manifest itself one snowdrop, one insight, one saint at a time. As its name might suggest, our Prime focuses on fundamentals.

Carrying out the counsel of St. Paul to "pray without ceasing" (1 Thessalonians 5:17), the Church sings all her daylight hours illumined by the Sun of Lauds. Our version of Prime continues a motif begun in Lauds: icons. Yet the concentration here is not on the icon as image of Christ Himself but as manifested in images of His saints, members of His Body extended throughout the ages.

Christian prayer is not "God and me," a cocoon-like embrace excluding everyone else. We have been instructed to address God as *our* Father. The ecclesial ark sails through the centuries bearing the remnant: us and our contemporaries, in company with all those of other eras, who together form Christ's mystical body.

How comforting to know that we need not be limited by our short span of years, our own abilities and accomplishments, or the geography of our temporal existence, but may borrow from the treasury accumulated by the Church in all the variety of her experience.

Made in the image of a God who is supremely interpersonal, we do not approach Him alone, but in company with His most holy Mother and all those who, throughout human history, have allowed His Holy Spirit to transform them.

> Remembering our most holy, most pure, most blessed and glorious Lady, Theotokos and ever-virgin Mary, with all the saints, let us commend ourselves and one another and our whole life to Christ our God.
>   To You, O Lord.
>   (THE DIVINE LITURGY OF ST. JOHN CHRYSOSTOM)

Flesh and blood that we are, though, we need more than words to bring these companions to life. Through the medium of the icon we see their faces glorified by the light of Christ; we sense the reality of them in their time, their holiness touching us in ours.

Holy Mother Church keeps them for us in all their particularity. Here is John the Baptist, in rags and with wild hair; St. Peter, white curls and beard framing his weathered fisherman's face; St. Mary of Egypt, scrawny and ascetic; or St. Paul, brown hair receding from the face of a Semitic scholar—all of them radiant with the trans-figuring life of Christ.

> How beautiful and comforting is the sight
> Of brethren who dwell together in unity!
> It's like precious balm poured on the head
> Till it drips down onto the beard;
> Running down Aaron's beard
> And over the collar of his tunic,
> As though dews of Hermon were
> Descending over the heights of Sion,
> Where the Lord gives His blessing:
> Everlasting life.
> (PSALM 133)

Prime teaches us that Mary, the Mother of God, is insep-arable from her Son. She, the flower of Israel, is the cul-mination of long centuries during which God endeavored to bring His people to understand His ways, and they to respond to Him. From Abraham to Moses, to Isaiah and Elijah, the Holy Spirit labors to reveal the Word, Icon of the Father, to His chosen people, tutoring them with His breath until there is Mary.

At last a woman so simply pure, so clear-eyed and faith-filled that she can respond to the Holy Spirit with her whole heart and conceive the Word! Through her *fiat* the whole human race becomes eligible for redemption, woman and man. As Christ is the new Adam, Mary is Eve transformed by grace, an Eve who gives birth, not to Cain and Abel, not to the conflict between good and evil, but to Christ, to wholeness.

Her icons depict her at the birth of Jesus, pointing to Him as the Way, cherishing Him as the focus of her life. They demonstrate how we too are called to give birth to Him in our flesh, to follow Him, allowing Him to be the Sun that illumines our life.

Like rainbow colors of fractured light, personalities of saints incarnate Christ over time in different places and through the varied circumstances of their lives. Their stories remind us of our own possibilities, inspiring us to respond to God, who calls us to Himself and thus to our true selves. Like windows into heaven, such images permit us glimpses of what is invisible but more real than what we see in this world.

Writing of the iconostasis, Pavel Florensky helps us to understand the role of the saints and their icons:

> [A] fog-cloud is a boundary between the visible and the invisible. It renders inaccessible to our weak sight that which it nevertheless reveals the real presence of; and once we open our spiritual eyes and raise them to the Throne of God, we contemplate heavenly visions: the cloud that covers the top of Mt.

Sinai, the cloud wherein the mystery of God's presence is revealed by that which clouds it. This cloud is
(in the Apostle's phrase) "a cloud of witnesses" (Heb.
12:1), it is the saints. . . . [T]hey are the "living stones"
that make up the living wall of the iconostasis, for
they dwell simultaneously in two worlds, combining
within themselves the life here and the life there. . . .
[F]or their holy countenances in themselves bear witness to the symbolic reality of their spiritual sight—
and, in them, the empirical crust is completely pierced
by light from above.[17]

In such company, how can we fail? Have we been
greater sinners than Mary Magdalene, Moses, Augustine,
or David? Are we weaker than Peter, more blind than
Paul before his encounter on the road to Damascus, or
than the disciples before Pentecost? Are we fishermen,
queens, learned or foolish? The transfigured faces of
saints of every description and walk of life are there for
us to encounter—and be encouraged.

In the Beatitudes we have descriptions of the "just
man," the saint. Through them God Himself shows us
how to distinguish the holy person and how to become
one ourselves.

Blessed are the poor in spirit; theirs is the Kingdom of
Heaven.

Blessed are those who mourn; they shall be comforted.

Blessed are the gentle; earth shall be their inheritance.

Blessed are those who hunger and thirst for holiness, for they shall be filled.

Blessed are those whose hearts have been purified; they shall see God.

Blessed are the peacemakers, for they shall be called Children of God.

Blessed are those who are persecuted in the cause of holiness: the Kingdom of Heaven is theirs.

Blessed are you when men revile you and persecute you and speak all manner of evil against you for My sake.

Rejoice and be exceedingly glad, for your reward will be great in heaven. It was thus that they persecuted the prophets who came before you.

(MATTHEW 5:3–12)

Prime teaches us not only to speak in prayer but also to listen, to better perceive. If we are becoming prayer, we're becoming capable of hearing the voice of God as it reaches us through the created world, through others, through Holy Scripture, from within our own hearts.

As we develop discernment, our ability to recognize the uncreated light in the faces of people around us also grows. Increasingly we view others as temples of the Holy Spirit, actual or potential, valuing them as we do our own lives, with ever-deepening conviction. For we are all meant to incarnate goodness, truth, and beauty in ways specific to us and our times, embodying Christ's healing and love for every age. Otherwise there would be no reason for the world to continue.

Prime celebrates the other. Inevitably, as the Kingdom of Heaven develops within us, the husk of self encapsulating its seed of divine life breaks open, allowing that life to actualize itself. "Unless the grain of wheat dies, itself remains alone" (John 12:24). Grain must die so that wheat may live; our alienated, self-centered selves must die so that the loving, divinized persons we are called to become may live.

Created in the image of God, who is not only supremely personal but *inter*personal, we're not actualizing that image, not truly in touch with and worshiping Him, unless we're also loving and serving our neighbor.

> You shall love the Lord your God
> With all your heart, with all your soul
> And with all your mind.
> This is the great and first commandment.
>
> And a second is like it:
> You shall love your neighbor as yourself.
> On these two commandments depend all the law and the
>   prophets.
> (MATTHEW 22:38–40)

These two commandments are in fact one. If our hearts are shuttered against the person who is easy to see, our neighbor dwelling with us in our own world, how can we pretend to be open to God, who, invisible, is more difficult to perceive? We have only one heart: open or closed. If that heart is truly open, it welcomes both our neighbor and the Holy Spirit of God. If it is closed, neither can enter.

By serving our sisters and brothers we manifest our love for One who has no need of our services. Loving the other as other—neither as an extension of ourselves nor as means to an end—is the mark of those who have learned love from the One who defines it, who *is* love.

Prime focuses our gaze on the great two-sided commandment: to love God in Himself and in His children. By the light of the risen Son who shows us how, and by the power of His Holy Spirit who makes us able, we can truly live it.

Praise the Lord!
It is good to sing praises to our God,
For He is beautiful and a song of praise is fitting.
The Lord builds up Jerusalem;
He brings home Israel's exiles;
He heals the broken-hearted, binding up their wounds.
Does He not number the stars, calling each by name?

How great is our Lord, how abundant His power!
How inscrutable His thinking!
The Lord sustains the afflicted, casting the impious to the
    dust.
Sing to the Lord with thanksgiving;
Make music to our God on the lyre!
He drapes the heavens with clouds.
He stores up rain for the earth,
Causing grass to spring up on the hills and plants for the
    use of man;
He provides pasture for cattle
And, for the young ravens who cry out, food.
He delights neither in the well-mounted warrior
Nor in the muscular runner.
The Lord's delight is in those who reverence Him,
Who hope in His merciful love.

Praise the Lord, O Jerusalem! Praise your God, O Zion!
For He strengthens the bolts of your gates,
Blessing your children within you.
He secures peace on your borders,
Filling you with the richest wheat.
He sends His word forth to the earth; how swiftly it runs!
He lets snow fall like wool, scattering hoarfrost like ashes.
He hurls hailstones like crumbs.
Who can withstand His cold?
He sends out His word, and all melts away,
Makes His wind blow and the waters flow.
He reveals His word to Jacob, His laws and decrees
    to Israel.

No other people has He treated this way
Or made known to them His will.
(PSALM 147)

But precisely how does Prime, with its emphasis on the other, relate to prayer? To "stand before God with our mind in our heart," gradually refining our knowledge and love of Him, opens us to the transforming action of His Holy Spirit. Little by little our being becomes unified, like the God we worship. With eyes on Him and our brothers and sisters, self-consciousness falls away. We become our prayer; we become love.

Some assert that all one need do "to be saved" is to give intellectual assent to dogmatic statements of belief. This perversion allows individuals to live lives indistinguishable from those of their pagan or agnostic fellow citizens except for an insurance policy: the statement that they believe what the Church believes. Put a nickel in the nickelodeon and out pops happily-ever-after.

The truth is that salvation, or being "saved," means being healed, becoming whole. It only happens as we perceive our Maker persistently revealing Himself day by day, hour after hour, to those with whom He longs to share true life.

The results of this kind of prayer are perceptible.

We undergo changes in our depths that gradually affect even the most superficial aspects of our being, as well as everyone with whom we come in contact. In some, such changes become so obvious that these people are universally acknowledged as saints.

The prophet Elijah is one of these. Icons of Elijah alone in the wilderness being fed by ravens show us the quintessential pray-er. Colorful episodes from his life have captured the imaginations of Jews and Christians alike, but neither fiery chariots nor miracles are the substance of the man.

The story of his sojourn at Mt. Horeb, which occurred more than eight hundred years before Christ, reveals an understanding of the subtlety of God's ways with us that rings just as true today.

> And word came to him: "Come out and stand on the mountain before the Lord; the Lord will be passing by."
> A great and mighty wind rent the mountains, crushing rocks before the Lord, but the Lord was not in the storm.
> And after the wind, an earthquake, but the Lord was not in the trembling of the earth.
> And after the earthquake, a fire, but the Lord was not in the fire.
> And after the fire, the whisper of a gentle breeze.

> When Elijah heard it, he covered his face with his
> mantle, came out, and stood at the entrance to the cave.
>
> Then a voice came to him, saying, "What are you
> doing here, Elijah?"
>
> (1 KINGS 19:11–13)

A twentieth-century icon, painted by Father Gregory Kroug, shows us St. Genevieve with long braids serenely holding a flaming candle in her right hand while she lifts her left, as if to stop one of the many would-be Parisian catastrophes she was able to avert.[18]

Simply through the power of the holiness of her life Genevieve was able to ease the sufferings of the Parisians during the city's occupation by the Franks. She had boatloads of food brought in for the people, secured the release of prisoners under both Childeric and Clovis, and in AD 451, foretold that Attila II and the Huns would bypass Paris. To this end, she led a campaign of prayer with her fellow citizens, and the city was not molested. She helped in the effort to build a church in honor of St. Denis, even persuading Clovis to build the church of Saints Peter and Paul.

How different from Elijah in time, place, and personality! Yet both share the profound inner life that unites a person with God; both possess the fearlessness before earthly power produced by viewing it in the perspective of eternity.

Lest we be tempted to relegate sanctity to the distant past, we have modern saints too numerous to list. Half-Russian, half-Aleut, St. Jacob of Alaska is known as the "Enlightener of the Native Peoples of Alaska." Born in 1802 on the Aleutian island of Atka, young Jacob Netsvetov decided to study for the priesthood at the Irkutsk Theological Seminary in eastern Siberia, but his desire to return to Atka led him back there in 1829. Six months after his arrival, he had performed sixteen baptisms, four hundred forty-two chrismations, fifty-three marriages, and eight funerals, celebrating the Divine Liturgy in a tent.[19]

This remarkable man collected and prepared specimens of marine animals and fish for museums in St. Petersburg and Moscow, corresponded with St. Innocent about linguistics and translating, worked on an Unangan-Aleut alphabet, and translated Scripture and other church writings for his people.

After the death of his wife Anna and the destruction of his house by fire, both in 1836, followed by the death of his father in 1837, St. Jacob petitioned his bishop for permission to return to Irkutsk to live as a monk. Bishop

Innocent, after his visit to Alaska and journey with St. Jacob to Kamchatka, apparently persuaded the young priest that his calling was to remain with the peoples of Alaska, since he did remain there the rest of his life.

Jacob worked with missionary zeal until he was no longer able, founding many more churches, inventing a new alphabet for the peoples of the Kuskokwim-Yukon Delta region, translating, and bringing the light of Christ to thousands.

When we contemplate the saints we should not overlook martyrs. There have been more martyrs in our time than in any other. People have been dying for their faith in huge numbers in China, Armenia, the Sudan, the old Soviet Union, India, Pakistan, Rwanda . . .

Prayer generates the kind of courage and fidelity exhibited by martyrs, a witness so powerful that it is often suppressed. The scope of contemporary martyrdom is only glimpsed piecemeal in reports that rarely, if ever, make the evening news.

The icon of the Forty Martyrs of Sebaste—soldiers who, in the year 320, under Constantine's pagan co-emperor Licinius, were frozen to death for their faith on an island in a lake near what is now Sivas in Turkey—is a powerful reminder of the witness of all martyrs.

Their story is more accessible than those of most early martyrs because the records we have are so close to the events they describe. Through these sources, we know of efforts made by Emperor Licinius's courts to bribe and threaten the soldiers to abandon their faith, and we know of the warm fires, bathhouse, and tables laden with good things to eat placed within their sight on the shores of the lake. Even a soldier who succumbed to the allure of the bathhouse is depicted in the icon, while written accounts relate his replacement by another soldier who was inspired by the thirty-nine faithful ones.

God is the "other" that Prime would have us envision, both in Himself and in our fellow humans. Saints represented in icons are those chosen to inspire us and our neighbors, but there are many saints among us whose faces are the only icons that will ever be painted of them.

As awareness of God's holiness grows, consciousness of our distance from that holiness, our relative lack of light, also grows. At the same time our humble perception of goodness, truth, and beauty in the people we meet deepens.

So does joy. "Joy is the echo of God's life in us," says Dom Marmion. St. Paul lists joy right after love as a fruit of the Holy Spirit: "But the fruit of the Spirit is love, *joy*, peace, patience, kindness, goodness, faithfulness, gentleness, self-control" (Galatians 5:22–23).

Joy is people like "Dan Sweep." Phone him for help with your recalcitrant chimney and a cheery voice with a strong Maine accent greets you:

> Spring is here
> And Dan is ready for another year,
> So put a big word in Dan's ear
> And he'll greet you with a great big cheer.
> Have no fear, he'll make sure your chimney's nice
>   and clear.
> Now you have a good day, you hear?

He arrives at your house and, in no time, what was mysterious about the chimney and its failings is so no longer. You and your chimney are on an intimate footing, what was broken is fixed for less than you expected, and Dan is off to make someone else's day.

Joy is Ann, wife, mother of three grown children, grandmother of eight. Her active spirit dances over the world she loves to explore, sharing her discoveries as she makes them. Faith generates the energy that fuels her inquiring mind, her service to others. She's a hospice volunteer. How many have had their last journey transformed by her loving care, her sense of humor, her silent prayers? Do they suspect she has MS?

Lauds provides us with Light to love by. Prime encourages us to take steps to stand in Him among our brothers and sisters, allowing Him to illumine everything we see. Then all we do is washed by the prayer that is love.

In 1980, I was invited to Pascha, the Orthodox Resurrection liturgy. From the choir loft I gazed down on the nave of a beautiful Russian church, its colorful walls and ceiling vivified by angels and saints garnered from past centuries.

The warm scent of honey from hundreds of beeswax tapers ascended on waves of music, as though the flow of time were being gradually irradiated by prayer. When the congregation turned to leave, to seek Christ's body in the darkness outside, I had no idea what they were doing.

Below me in the shadowy nave streamed a river of reverent faces, each illumined by the glowing candle beneath it. The river flowed, the singing swelled as hundreds of lit faces surged toward the doors. I saw Holy Tradition as the communion of saints: one radiant river of faces rippling down the centuries.

Like the Great Commandment, our image for Prime is a diptych. A "Seder" at the Catholic church in Rockland, Maine, inspired the other half.

Across the supper table, Robert Carter was describing another river, the Una, which flows south from the slopes of the Strazbenica Mountain in Bosnia to Jasenovac in Croatia. His first views of it were as he drove along a road high above the riverbed.

Fascinated by brilliant, jewel-like colors flashing up at him—exquisite reds, blues, purples, and greens—he realized, when down at the level of the river, that they were merely stones and plants in the riverbed intensified by the incredible clarity, the extraordinary purity of the water flowing over them.

Are these pictures framed, like their predecessors? Yes. It's a simple frame of water rippling like a sparkling stream, encircling each image and joining them. All the colors of earth are baptized in the elusive identity of the river. Is it the Jordan? Or the river One: *Una*?

Or an image of the Holy Spirit?

TIERCE
THIRD HOUR

"But the hour is coming and is now here when true worshipers will worship the Father in spirit and in truth. For it is such worshippers the Father seeks. God is spirit, and those who worship Him must worship in spirit and in truth."

JOHN 4:23–24

At nine o'clock in late April one hardly expects to be wadded by snow into winter silence eighteen inches deep. Nor could one have conceived the sweetness of bewildered birds weaving their chirps and twitters, like singing garlands, above the draped whites of a smothered landscape. Which only serves to remind one of the Wisdom that did conceive it.

Nine o'clock is Tierce, a practical, getting-down-to-business hour perfect for shoveling unexpected snow or considering the relation of prayer to prayers. If we always keep in mind St. Theophan's definition, "Prayer is standing before God with our mind in our heart," the distinction will be of little moment. For, whether our prayer is wordless or expressed in language, and whether that language is our own or another's, the essence is still the same.

Prayers are necessary, though, especially as we take our early steps in the art of communicating with God. Westerners persuaded of the superiority of "creativity" over memorization tend to place more value on spontaneous utterance than their Eastern brethren. Yet both spontaneity and adherence to well-worn forms of antiquity have roles in the tutelage of one who would progress in prayer.

Of course we must be able to express ourselves in our own words. Little effort need be expended to convince us of that. But persuasion may be required for us to appreciate the value of prayers composed by others. For that we must wean ourselves from valuing our own words simply because they are ours.

When we employ words they're like boats carrying the expression of our hearts to God. It matters more that they are good boats than that *we* built them, particularly if we aren't skilled.

They need not be eloquent. Eloquence can often get in the way, focusing awareness on self rather than on the One to whom we pray. Have you ever been awestruck by the ability of someone praying aloud spontaneously, only to realize afterward that your attention had been fixated on the "boat" rather than on God?

The river of Holy Tradition celebrated in Prime belongs to us. Like fish, we swim in its living waters and nourish ourselves on the spiritual food we discover in its depths. We adopt prayers in Scripture as our own, borrow parts of the Liturgy, keep company with the most profound minds, the most remarkable performers on the stage of history. All of it bears us, if we let it, to the One Father, Son, and Holy Spirit, who summons us to His Kingdom, His more abundant life, Himself.

Since the psalms are the basis of the Church's hours, learning to pray them, making them our own, is one of the best ways to grow into pray-ers. Prayers of saints belong to us too. Creating a "rule of prayer" for ourselves, instilling the habit of praying at certain times, usually means appropriating from this treasury what suits our needs.

The sign of the cross, made with attention, draws us into awareness of God at the same time that it covers us with the emblem of Christ's paschal victory and the embrace of the Trinity. We begin and end prayers with it or make it before eating or drinking. It can be the first thing we do when we wake and the last before we shut our eyes. So simple, but an effective way to make the transition between this world and the Kingdom of God.

An obvious opportunity for borrowed prayer is mealtime. When we gather to eat, we ask a blessing on the food and return thanks for it. I love to use a variation on words from Psalm 104, the Vespers psalm:

> The eyes of all look hopefully to You, O Lord,
> To give them their food in due season.
> You provide; we gather.
> You open Your hand and fill every living creature
> With good things.
> You send forth Your Spirit; we are created afresh
> And You renew the face of the earth.
> Bless this food to Your service.
> Amen.

When I pray this prayer I see eyes of forest animals gazing up toward someone about to feed them, of goldfish as they swim to the surface of their bowl hoping for the little crumbs they so desire. We, like them, depend on the One who gives us, not merely food to sustain life, but life itself.

From the preface to the Holy Anaphora comes a prayer suitable for any time:

> It is meet and right that we should sing of You,
> Bless You, praise You, give thanks unto You
> And adore You in all places of Your dominion.
> For You are God indescribable,
> Incomprehensible, invisible, inconceivable;
> Forever existing, forever the same;
> You, with Your only-begotten Son and Your Holy Spirit.
> From nothingness You called us into being,
> And when we had fallen away from You,
> You raised us again, leaving nothing undone
> Until You could lead us to heaven
> And bestow on us Your Kingdom which is to come.
> For all these things we give thanks to You
> And Your only begotten Son and Your Holy Spirit:
> For all the things whereof we know
> And those whereof we know not,
> For all benefits bestowed upon us,
> Both the manifest and the unseen.

Much has been written about the "Jesus prayer."[20] For many it has been the elevator lifting and keeping them aware of the presence of God. It is not, as some may think, a Christian version of "Om," although both are repeated and both take over space in one's mind, keeping other things out.

"Om" is a sound without meaning or content. The Jesus prayer is full of meaning: "Lord Jesus Christ, Son of God, have mercy on me, a sinner." Simple as it is, the prayer acknowledges Jesus Christ as Lord, putting Him first and self last. In it we ask for His mercy, since the bottom line of our relation to God is that it rests on His merciful willingness to forgive, not on our virtue or achievements. Mother Maria (Skobtsova) of Paris wrote:

> The Jesus prayer helps to lift the whole life, body and soul, to a level where senses and imagination no longer seek for outward change or stimulation, where all is subordinated to the one aim of centering the whole attention of body and soul upon God in the sense that the world is sought and known in the beauty of God, not God in the beauty of the world.[21]

Doing the Jesus prayer is the only way to understand it. Praying it with as much attention as one possesses will not only deepen our awareness of the presence of God and shape our humility, it will instruct our mind about the prayer itself. We'll come to see how valuable it can be for moments of mental vacancy that might be wasted in trivial, vain, or unwanted thoughts.

Like a rudder, the prayer steers us toward God in the midst of the temporal flotsam and jetsam competing for our attention. This humble instrument is capable of still-ing and concentrating our distractible hearts. And when we're praying for others, how easily we "become" those for whom we pray, inserting them in the place we ordi-narily occupy at the end of the sentence.

At first blush, "pray always" may seem to require the monotony of a steady-state consciousness imposing itself on our life experiences. In reality, prayer, like the River Una, vivifies those experiences in all their variety and uniqueness, revealing the knobby shapes and subtle colors of each in ways inaccessible to ordinary percep-tion. Everything is an occasion for prayer. Every moment can provoke us to praise, delight, gratitude, penitence, acknowledgment of our dependence.

As we digest Holy Scripture and the Liturgy, phrases reverberate in our minds. When I sing the Greek Divine Liturgy, lilting melodies of certain lines chase my thoughts during the week. *"Evlogitos ei, Kyrie, didaxon me ta dikaiomata Sou"* ("Blessed are You, O Lord, teach me Your statutes") from the Great Doxology is one of these. At a time when I was making a major decision, "If today you hear His voice, harden not your heart" from Psalm 95 sprang into my mind and ran through it for days.

"'For My thoughts are not your thoughts, nor are your ways My ways,' says the Lord. 'High as the heavens are above the earth, so high are My thoughts above yours'" (Isaiah 55:8–9) is another of these brief reminders. In high school, a lovely musical setting of the Angelus found its way into my personal prayer, especially the *"Ecce ancilla Domini, fiat mihi secundum verbum Tuum"* ("Behold the handmaid of the Lord, be it done unto me according to Your word"). Just saying, "Glory to You, O Lord, glory to You," when we wake up can orient our day. These are samples of thousands one might employ to illustrate the way simple sentences can thread the day with prayer.

Psalms are not the only source of prayer in Scripture. The Canticle of Hezekiah offers us prayer that is a poignant meditation on death:

> In the noontime of life I must depart!
> The gates of the nether world shall enclose me
> For the remainder of my years.
> No more will I see the Lord
> In the land of the living, thought I,
> No longer see even one face
> Among those who inhabit the world.
> My dwelling is snatched from me,
> Folded up like a shepherd's tent.
> The Weaver who knit my life
> Severs the threads on the loom.
> Day reaches evening:

You are putting an end to me.
All night long I lie still, sobbing until morning,
As though a lion had broken my bones.
Day reaches evening: You are finishing me.
I peep like a swallow, moan like a dove;
My eyes weary from gazing toward heaven.
Lord, I am overwhelmed; help me!
Yet how can I speak, and what do I say to Him
When it is He who acts?
With bitterness of heart I review my years.
Lord, in such paltry things men's life consists;
In these is the life of my spirit.
Oh, heal me! Make me live!
Now my bitterness changes into well-being!
You have preserved my soul from oblivion,
Thrusting my sins behind You.
For You receive no praise from the nether world;
It is not the dead who honor You.
Those who go down to the pit
No longer hope in Your faithfulness.
It is the living who give You thanks as I do today,
Father handing on to son the story of Your fidelity.
Lord, come to my aid, and all the days of our life
We will make music in Your house with harps.
(ISAIAH 38:10–20)

If the Church is the ark, composed prayers might be seen as lifeboats. They are an aspect of the communion of saints in the sense that, when we need them, when our own prayer seems inadequate or inexpressive, prayers of our brothers and sisters in faith can come to the rescue, unimpeded by separation in time.

Prayers are like framing for a house. They provide structure and form, marking times for prayer which, without such markers, can dissolve into nothingness before the press of daily events and cares.

Little has been said about the prayer of petition. It may be the most common form prayer takes because human beings are so naturally inclined to want something, or to see petition as a form of manipulation of the Divine. (If we pray hard enough God will do *our* bidding!) Petitioning God is actually acknowledging our true relationship to Him as dependents.

Our instruction manual, the Lord's Prayer, illustrates the sorts of requests Christ encourages: that God's name be revered, that the Kingdom of God may come among us, that the Father's will be done on earth as in heaven. After these most important petitions, we make a personal one: that we be given sustenance for our life so we can accomplish what we have just requested.

For we're not passively begging God to act but asking for His Holy Spirit so that His designs for the world may be brought about in and through us. The Kingdom comes into this world through our personal transformation.

Ancient Israelites understood that when they asked for God's blessing, they were asking Him to give *them* the power to accomplish what they desired. We pray in this same spirit.

Immediately after he presents the Lord's Prayer in his Gospel, St. Luke appends a commentary by its Author. The true object of our prayers of petition is disclosed in the last verse of this commentary: "If you who are evil know how to give good gifts to your children, how much more will the heavenly Father give the Holy Spirit to those who ask Him?" (Luke 11:13).

Once we have really acknowledged Christ as the Sun of our universe, as the revelation of the Father, our Christian life becomes oriented toward transformation in Him to achieve the fulfillment of our nature. Such transformation doesn't occur as a result of piling up gold stars on a celestial chart or merit badges for our good deeds. Theosis is only accomplished through the Holy Spirit. Our task then, the ultimate object of our petitions, is to allow the Holy Spirit to increase within us.

> Unless the Lord builds the house,
> They labor in vain who build it.
> Unless the Lord watches over the city,
> Vain is the watchman's vigil.
> (PSALM 127:1)

St. Francis's well-loved prayer of petition, composed in the spirit of the Lord's Prayer, is one millions have made their own:

Lord, make me an instrument of Your peace.
Where there is hatred, let me sow love,
Where there is injury, pardon,
Where there is doubt, faith,
Where there is despair, hope,
Where there is darkness, light,
And where there is sadness, joy.
O Divine Master,
Grant that I may not so much seek
To be consoled as to console;
To be understood as to understand;
To be loved as to love;
For it is in giving that we receive;
It is in pardoning that we are pardoned,
And it is in dying that we are born to eternal life.

Many like to employ one of the earliest Christian hymns as their evening prayer. Translated as "O Gladsome Light," it's the ancient Vespers hymn: *Phos Hilaron*. The Greek is closer to "O Joyous Radiance," the "joyous" so full that it borders on hilarity.

Gathering the day's light into concentrated color before disappearing, the setting sun is a symbol of Christ summing up all creation in Himself as He simultaneously reflects the glorious face of the Father hidden in the night of our unknowing. In the same way, *Phos Hilaron* distills the sunsets and Vespers of two thousand years to enrich our prayer with their patina.

The prayer of St. Ephraim, recited by Orthodox each day during Lent, need not be restricted to them or to that time of year:

> Lord, Master of my life, take from me the spirit of sloth, faint-heartedness, lust for power, and idle words.
>
> Grant me instead the spirit of humility, chastity, patience, and love.
>
> Yes, Lord, grant that I may see my own sins and not see my brothers', for Thou art blessed from all ages to all ages. Amen.

Performing a prostration after each petition deepens the prayer, drawing flesh and blood into it as no mere recitation of words can.

> I will sing of steadfast love and justice;
> For You, O Lord, I will play music.
> I will walk in the way of the blameless.

Oh, when will You come to me?
Here, within my house, I will walk
With integrity of heart,
Setting before my eyes nothing that is vile.
I hate the ways of those who fall away;
They shall have no power over me.
Far from me the perverse of heart;
The impious I disown.
Whoever slanders his neighbor secretly I will silence.
Whoever has a haughty eye and an arrogant heart
I will not endure.
I will look with favor on the faithful in the land
That they may dwell with me;
Only one who walks in the way of perfection
Shall be my servant.
No one who practices deceit shall dwell in my house;
Nor shall one who utters lies remain in my presence.
Morning by morning I will silence all the impious in
        the land,
Uprooting evildoers from the city of the Lord.
(PSALM 101)

Our miniature for Tierce? Let's start with the frame. It's a *Deisis* of sorts, Christ in a *mandorla* (geometric surround indicating the heavenly dimension) at the top. To his right and left are saints from an icon screen inclining their heads toward Him. Down the sides cascade images of mice, robins, boars, goldfish, lions, owls, kittens, and porpoises, eyes all lifted toward Christ. Along the bottom dance daffodils, tulips, anemones, their faces too turned upward toward the mandorla.

Within the frame there is stillness and movement. The formidable stone backdrop is the Wailing Wall in Jerusalem, warmed by golden sun. Black-hatted Orthodox Jews nod their heads rhythmically toward it, deep in concentration as they read their prayers. In the foreground walks an old woman in black, silently fingering her rosary.

Sext

Sixth Hour

It was now about the sixth hour when the sun was eclipsed and darkness fell over the whole land until the ninth hour.

LUKE 23:44–45

nd darkness fell over the whole land"—in the middle of the day. As far as this world is concerned, its light went out when Jesus gave up His spirit. Out of that darkness, from the parched lips of a sadistically beaten virtual corpse suspended by nails from a wooden cross, came the deepest prayer ever uttered by man: "Father, forgive them. They know not what they do."

> He whom none may touch is seized;
> He who looses Adam from the curse is bound.
> He who tries the hearts and inner thoughts

Of man is unjustly brought to trial;
He who closed the abyss is shut in prison.
He before whom the powers of heaven stand
With trembling stands before Pilate;
The Creator is struck by the hand of His creature.
He who comes to judge the living and the dead
Is condemned to the cross;
The destroyer of hell is enclosed in a tomb.
O You who endure all these things in Your tender love,
Who have saved all men from the curse,
O longsuffering Lord, glory to You.
(FROM VESPERS ON GREAT FRIDAY)

Sext, though beginning at noon, is dark, darker than Matins, precisely because the Sun has come. The predawn darkness anticipated light; this darkness has rejected it. This is the darkness of sin, death, and spiritual blindness.

The middle of the day, the time of crucifixion, is a traditional symbol for *akedia*, the "noonday devil" that seeks to devour us through our sloth, our willingness to be distracted by cares, boredom, and triviality from the "one thing necessary." It's the hour when the sheer volume of happenings reinforces our reluctance to "seek first the kingdom of God," or when negative forces appear overwhelming.

Yet if we penetrate to the heart of even this darkness we find the cross. Invisible to those without faith, for the believer the cross is capable of changing a fearful dark into the comforting "shadow of the Most High." "Even should I walk through the valley of the shadow of death, I will fear no evil, for You are with me" (Psalm 23:4).

> He who abides in the mystery of the Most High
> Dwells in the shadow of the Almighty,
> Saying to the Lord: "My refuge, my fortress,
> My God on whom I depend."
> He will snatch you from the snare of the fowler,
> Whose business is to destroy you;
> He covers you with His wings;
> Under His pinions you shall find refuge;
> His truth, your shield and buckler.
> You shall not fear the terrors of night
> Nor the arrow that flies by day;
> Neither pestilence stalking in darkness
> Nor devastating boredom at noon.
> A thousand may fall at your side,
> Ten thousand at your right hand,
> But you remain untouched.
> It is enough for your eyes to see
> The punishment of the impious.
> Because you say, "The Lord is my refuge,"
> And make the Most High your dwelling-place,
> Evil shall not dissolve you,
> Nor shall plague prowl near your tent.
> He has given His angels charge over you
> To keep you in all your ways.

They shall bear you up in their hands
Lest you dash your foot against a stone.
(PSALM 91:1–12)

Although we know the next chapter in the story, it's critical to meditate on Christ's Passion without reference to what follows. How else absorb the height and depth and breadth of the love of God? How else understand what Christ's mother, the apostles and disciples of Christ felt during that dark time?

When Jesus died, so did all hope in Him as Messiah. It now appeared that His preaching, His wisdom, all the truths He taught, were illusions snuffed out by death. Each disciple must have scoured his mind and spirit, almost doubting his own existence. How could they have been so deluded?

But had they been? Surely Jesus *was* truth. Nothing had so satisfied their hearts as the words He spoke, His calm, confident presence among them. But He was dead.... Our personal impasses, our moments of discouragement, cannot hold a candle to theirs. They had not the comfort of knowing the sequel.

Prayerfully reading Gospel accounts of the Passion, stopping wherever understanding deepens, is essential if we are to learn Christ. God wishes to be known by us, known in the biblical sense of intimate love and relation. Such knowing is the life of unending delightful revelation for which He created us but, because of our history of infidelity and the world's irreversible rejection of Christ, it cannot be found apart from the cross. Varieties of Christian faith that avert their eyes from the crucifixion are pale aberrations producing a pasty, effeminate Jesus who is the high priest of niceness, of that bloodless rectitude guilty of spawning generations of atheists.

If the first reason for meditation on the Passion is to deepen our knowledge of who Christ is and to what lengths God was prepared to go so that we might share His life, the second has to do with our own "passion." Whatever our suffering, we know that He has gone before us. He, the sinless one, with a capacity for pain infinitely beyond ours, has faced and conquered suffering and death—even the death of the cross.

Early in the fourth century, Emperor Constantine outlawed crucifixion and, during the same period, legitimized Christianity. Christians came forth out of the shadows, emerging from catacombs and houses where they had gathered for worship, to begin building churches. The cross, no longer merely a symbol of the most degrading, tortured form of execution, moved from hidden veneration to the public square. There it was exalted as the sign of Christ's victory over sin and death.

If Christ is the "Way, the Truth, and the Life," His cross is the signpost. Without it we cannot find the Way, discover the Truth, or live as God means us to live. The cross, at the heart of our lives as Christians, is *ipso facto* the heart of our prayer.

"Unless the seed die, itself remains alone." Unless "I" is able to break out of "me"; unless the hard casing around the germ of true life residing within us as God's image is destroyed, we remain alone: blind, self-centered, aborted seeds of persons we never became.

Breaking the shell hurts. Many hammer blows are needed to destroy it. But destruction of this shell, of all that impedes our growth in the Holy Spirit, is the true basis for asceticism and the words of Jesus:

> If anyone would come after Me, let him deny himself and take up his cross and follow Me. For whoever would save his life will lose it, but whoever loses his life for My sake will find it. For what will it profit a man if he gains the whole world and forfeits his own life? Or what shall a man give in return for his life?
>
> (MATTHEW 16:24–26)

What does it mean to "deny himself and take up his cross"? Do we run about seeking to rub unpleasantness into our lives at every turn? No, because that would still be self-will perverting the goodness of the life we've been given, focusing on unpleasantness rather than on God. There is no need to seek the cross. It finds us.

The cross is a powerful symbol of the tension between God's ways and ours. When they coincide, tension between the vertical (divine) and horizontal (human) arms of the cross disappears. God, in taking our flesh, has done His part by bending the vertical beam. We must do ours, yielding up our self-will to the One who emptied Himself to heal us with His love.

In the Lord's Prayer, at the moment of the Incarnation, during the agony in the Garden, we have examples of perfect alignment:

> "Thy will be done on earth as it is in heaven."
> (MATTHEW 6:10)

> "Behold the handmaid of the Lord; be it unto me according to thy word."
> (LUKE 1:38)

> "My Father, if this cup cannot pass unless I drink it, may Thy will be done!"
> (MATTHEW 26:42)

Often misinterpreted as a cry of despair, Christ's words spoken from the cross, "My God, my God, why have

You forsaken Me?" (Matthew 27:46), are the first line of
a well-known messianic psalm that foretells aspects of
Messiah's death and expresses ultimate triumph in the
midst of apparently overwhelming disaster.

> My God, my God, why have You forsaken me?
> Why are the words I groan so far from saving me?
> O my God, I cry by day, but You do not answer;
> By night, and hear only silence.
> Yet You are the Holy, enthroned on the praises of Israel.
> In You our fathers put their faith;
> They trusted, and You set them free.
> To You they cried and were rescued;
> In You they placed their confidence and were not put
>   to shame.
> But I, a worm and no man, am the laughing-stock of the
>   people,
> Despised by the crowd.
> All who see me mock me; they wag their heads and sneer:
> "He trusted the Lord, let Him deliver him!
> Let Him set His favorite free!"
> Yet You are He who drew me from the womb,
> Whom I have trusted from my mother's breast.
> To You was I committed from my birth,
> And from my mother's womb You have been my God.
> Be not far from me when the agony of death is near
> And there is no one to help.
> Many bulls surround me; strong bulls of Bashan
>   encircle me;

At me their jaws gape like voracious and roaring lions.

I am poured out like water, and all my bones are
dislocated;

My heart, like wax, is melted within my breast.

My throat is as dry as baked clay, and my tongue sticks to
my jaws;

You have laid me in the dust to die.

Like a pack of circling dogs, a gang of ruffians surrounds me;

They have pierced my hands and my feet—I can count
all my bones;

The people gloat, staring at me.

They divide my garments among them, casting lots for
my cloak.

But You, O Lord, be not far away!

O my strength, come quickly to help me!

Deliver my soul from the sword,

My precious life from the clutches of the dog!

Save me from the jaws of the lion, my poor soul from the
bull's horn!

I will proclaim Your name to my brothers;

In the great assembly I will praise You:

"You who fear the Lord, praise Him!

All you offspring of Jacob, glorify Him

And stand in awe of Him, all you descendants of Israel!

For He has neither slighted nor disdained the poverty of
the poor one,

Nor hidden His face from me, but heard me when He was
invoked."

From You comes my praise in the great assembly;

My vows I will fulfill before His worshipers.
The poor shall eat and have their fill;
Those who seek Him shall praise the Lord!
May your hearts live forever!
All the ends of the earth shall remember and come back
 to the Lord;
All the heathens shall bow down before Him.
For kingship belongs to the Lord, who rules all the
 earth.
Yes! Before Him alone all the powerful of the earth shall
 bow down;
All who go down to the dust shall humble themselves
 before Him,
And the descendants of those who live no longer shall
 serve Him.
They will proclaim the Lord in the ages to come,
Telling a people yet unborn of His faithfulness:
"Hear what He has done!"
(PSALM 22)

The cross comes to us without our seeking it. One might even say it dwells in the depths of our being, where the battle between what we are and who we are being called to be takes place. Our task is to embrace its manifestations, allowing them to break us open, to smelt us in the furnace of suffering, purging dross from the gold of experience, gradually weaning us from this passing life as the imperishable one develops within us.

Taking up the cross is permitting our illnesses, misfortunes, and losses, the irritating ways of those about us (as well as our own)—our dying—to sculpt us, cutting away what obscures the likeness of God that shapes us from within.

Endeavoring to submit ourselves to the Church's schedule of fasting is also part of taking up the cross. Fasting, like prayer, reminds us of the presence of God and helps us harmonize our bodies with our spirits. Nor is our fasting limited to food and drink. We must abstain from all that draws us away from God, whether that is overwork, self-absorption, entertainment incompatible with Christ, addictions, compulsions—whatever in our particular life obstructs the life of God in us.

The simple truth is that we cannot grow, the seed cannot even germinate, unless we embrace the suffering intrinsic to our lives, seeing each instance as a gift from our loving Father. It's a long journey from dust to divinity. Transformation of created, finite, wounded humans cannot occur without stretching: the cross.

In our pilgrimage to God, the nexus of the cross is conforming our will to His. All asceticism can be summed up in that concept. Learning to see as God does—putting on "the mind of Jesus Christ," accepting what goes against the grain—turns adversity into fuel, into love.

Theoretical? Not when we see it in the joyful eyes of an amputee wheeling himself across a Chicago street, gratitude for the gift of life radiating in his smile. Who has not marveled at the heroic selflessness of a wife nursing her sick husband, day in, day out, year in, year out, with no resentment for the "waste" of her life, no reference to her "needs," her "fulfillment"? And what of those who have transformed prison sentences into spiritual freedom? Such examples are figures of the resurrection that follows every embrace of the cross.

How is suffering prayer? Often we neglect to pray when things go well, when great health and good fortune veil the transitory nature of earthly existence, distracting us from its purpose—theosis: our transformation from dust to divinity.

But nothing inspires deep prayer so surely as the sense that waves are closing over our heads, that we've been backed into a corner by "our adversaries," whether these are our own flawed judgment, others' ill-will, calamity, loss of a loved one, or the diminishments of ill health. At such times even hardened sinners may "stand before God with their mind in their hearts."

Many, if not most, psalms owe their inspiration to a desperate situation:

Out of the depths have I cried to You, O Lord; Lord, hear
my prayer.
(PSALM 130:1)

Give ear to my words, O Lord; consider my groaning.
(PSALM 5:1)

O Lord my God, in You I take refuge; save me from all my
pursuers and deliver me.
(PSALM 7:1)

Why, O Lord, do You stand far off? Why do You hide
Yourself in times of trouble?
(PSALM 10:1)

I waited patiently for the Lord; He inclined to me and
heard my cry. He drew me up from the pit of destruction, out of the miry bog.
(PSALM 40:1–2)

This sort of prayer is really faith in action. Instead
of despairing, the faithful turn to the "Giver of Life,"
the "Treasury of blessing," who alone has power to help
them.

Faith untried is a wrapped gift. Adversity embraced
unwraps it. In every instance those we revere for their
great faith have been proven in the purifying fire of
adversity.

Our father Abraham left the familiar trappings of his life in Ur of the Chaldees to follow where God led him. When God assured him in his old age that his barren wife would conceive a son and he would father a multitude of nations, Sarah laughed. But Abraham believed because God said it would be so. And when the child born to them, Isaac (Laughter!), was nearly full-grown, God tried Abraham's faith again.

> "Take your son, your only son Isaac whom you love: go to the land of Moriah and offer him there as a burnt offering on one of the mountains of which I shall tell you." . . .
>
> And Isaac said to his father Abraham, "My father? And he said, "Yes, my son?"
>
> He said, "Behold the fire and the wood, but where is the lamb? For a burnt offering?"
>
> Abraham said, "God will provide for Himself the lamb for a burnt offering, my son."
>
> (GENESIS 22:2, 7–8)

Abraham's prayer—absolute trust and conformity to the will of God despite every appearance to the contrary—is what made him the father of Israel and a model for the faithful of every generation.

Moderns who consider themselves more evolved than their *Habiru* (Hebrew) forebears may find this story difficult. The thought of child sacrifice is abhorrent. Even more abhorrent is the idea of God's commanding it. But if we place a few more thought-pieces into our prayer kaleidoscope, turning it to change their relationship to one another, perhaps a satisfying pattern will emerge.

In the first place, *we* practice child sacrifice. By aborting them, we sacrifice our children to the gods of sexual promiscuity, material comfort, and convenience rather than to Baal.

This removes us from the mountaintop of moral superiority and deposits us firmly in the lowly camp of Abraham's neighbors, the Canaanites. Yet even though child sacrifice is common among us, we have yet to fully convince ourselves that it's a good thing. In fact, we know it's not, and thus we recoil in horror at the thought of God's requesting it.

Abraham dwelt, not in a world illumined by the light of the gospel, but in the predawn darkness of Matins, lit only by the slender taper of his individual faith. Israel would not even come into existence until his grandson Jacob had children. If Abraham's neighbors' way of worshiping was to sacrifice to an idol what they considered most precious, would Abraham be shocked if Yahweh, who was no idol but the One Who Is, required as much?

God had shown Himself faithful in the past. He

promised Abraham a son who would make him patriarch of "a multitude of nations" although Sarah was barren and he, ninety-nine. Impossible? It came to pass.

Now Abraham is asked to sacrifice the only means through which God's promise of a "multitude of nations" can be fulfilled. But who is he to question God's ways, even when they seem to contradict his own experience of those ways? Abraham lived near the beginning of the long process of learning God, yet he understood something we are slow to grasp: God, who created all, has absolute jurisdiction over birth and death and everything in between.

Ultimately, God did not require the sacrifice, revealing something about Himself as well as about Abraham's faith. But, had the Lord required it, Abraham was aware that he had not been consulted at the world's creation, nor was he privy to God's ways and thoughts, so far above ours. Abraham submitted his judgment and will to the Lord, who made, not only him and all creation, but all the "rules."

The story of Job underscores the same point. It takes Job a while to disentangle himself from reliance on his own good deeds, his own righteousness; he questions his Maker from the perspective of finitude.

Then the Lord answered Job out of the whirlwind
  and said:
"Who is this that clouds the truth of things
With ill-considered words?
Gird up your loins like a man;
I will question you, and you answer Me:
Where were you when I laid the foundations of the earth?
Tell Me, if you have understanding,
Who determined its measurements? Surely you know!
Or who stretched the line upon it?
On what were its bases sunk,
Or who laid the cornerstone
When the morning stars sang together
And all the sons of God shouted for joy?"
(JOB 38:1–7)

After a lengthy divine tutorial, Job humbles himself, accepting whatever God has decreed:

"I have uttered what I did not understand,
Things too wonderful for me, which I did not know. . . .

"I had heard of You by the hearing of the ear,
But now my eye sees You;
Therefore I despise myself
And repent in dust and ashes."
(JOB 42:3, 5)

When, by the light of the cross, we say, "now my eye sees You; therefore I despise myself and repent," we have truly reached the point of *metanoia*, change of heart.

From the cross everything falls into perspective: Time flows toward the cross and from it. We begin to see the purpose of creation, of our own life. Without this perspective a person's deepest cry is that of the Preacher: "Vanity of vanities, all is vanity" (Ecclesiastes 1:2), and the limited, transitory nature of earthly pleasure erupts in the words of the popular song, "Is that all there is?"

At the juncture of the cross, the place where divine and human coincide, tension between them is resolved when we align our human wills with God's. Doing this usually requires going against our inclinations, especially at the outset. Fasting, giving to the poor, doing small kindnesses or visiting the sick and imprisoned are all ways of conquering oneself in favor of God and our fellow human beings. "He must increase, but I must decrease" (John 3:30); the seed must die so that the life within can manifest itself, push up through the dark earth and flourish in the light.

Is it accidental that John the Baptist, the great preacher of *metanoia* who prepared the path for Messiah, is placed prominently near the beginning of all four Gospels? That he nearly always occupies the place to Christ's left on the icon screen? That each year he is celebrated with four feasts on the church calendar?

Holy Mother Church understands that without asceticism we simply do not enter the Kingdom. Just as John the Baptist prepared his followers for Messiah and provided Christ with a body of disciples already partially "catechized," asceticism—self-denial—is the necessary forerunner to Christ's life maturing in us.

Christ was crucified for being who He was. His followers may expect the same fate, or something analogous. For at the heart of our being, at the confluence of divine and human in us, where the image of God resides and His likeness is being forged, the cross will manifest itself, pushing at our "shell" from within as contrary forces bruise it from without.

Sext invites us to Christ's Passion to meditate, to contemplate. There we will learn to recognize our own cross and receive the strength to shoulder it. Are we unable to carry its full weight? Why then, let us bear what we can. The glorious surprise is that, embraced, it's always lighter than we thought. Here it may be well to listen to the words of Evagrius, writing on prayer and the spiritual life:

> Anyone who wishes to embark on the labors of the virtuous life should train himself gently until he finally

reaches the perfect state. Do not be perplexed by the many paths trodden by our Fathers of old, each different from the other; do not zealously try to imitate them all: this would only upset your way of life. Rather choose a way of life that suits your feeble state; travel on that and you will live, for your Lord is merciful and He will receive you, not because of your achievements, but because of your intention, just as He received the gift of the destitute woman.[22]

This counsel is like St. Augustine's joke: "Love God and do what you will." For if we truly love God, truly embark on the virtuous life, we won't remain long in the "feeble state," and what we will becomes identical to what God wills.

When confronted by evil, when horrified by the slaughter of human beings, by corruption, by our own failures, when pushed to the limits, we contemplate the Crucified, remembering that He faced all this before us and conquered. At such times it is well to remember the parable of the weeds:

> The Kingdom of Heaven may be compared to a man who sowed good seed in his field, but while his men were sleeping, his enemy came and sowed weeds among the wheat and went away. So when the plants came up and bore grain, then the weeds also appeared.

And the servants of the master of the house came and said to him, "Master, did you not sow good seed in your field? How then does it have weeds?" He said to them, "An enemy has done this." So the servants said to him, "Then do you want us to go and gather them?" But he said, "No, lest in gathering up the weeds you root up the wheat along with them. Let both grow together until the harvest, and at harvest time I will tell the reapers: 'Gather the weeds first and bind them in bundles to be burned. Then gather the wheat into my barn.'"

(MATTHEW 13:24–30)

We might also recall Christ's most frequent admonitions—"Fear not" and "Peace be with you"—repeated so often in the Gospels that they must be the words we most need to hear.

During Easter season, when we shout, *"Christos Anesti!"* "Christ is Risen!" we express the certainty that however horrendous evil seems in this life, it is nothing compared to the joys of the life to come. Evil passes; these joys do not.

More than that. God knew that it was *worth* the crucifixion of His Son to allow us a share in His life. God thought it worth risking all the horrors of which the perverted human will is capable to create beings who could *choose* to love, could *will* to allow love to leaven their existence until love *became* their existence. Isn't this the fullness of prayer?

Bristol, Vermont, December, 1984. Tattered remnants of early evening sky have dissipated, supplanted by an enveloping, cold blackness occasionally pierced by lit windows. My son and I are on our way to pick up the Christmas wreath. We stop at a tiny house clinging to its bank high above the rushing waters of the New Haven River. So united are bank and house that the river might have given birth to this minute dwelling, hurtling it to its lofty perch, where it stuck, then rooted: a halfway house between river and woods.

The roar of water surrounding us at the door follows us inside to mingle with incense of freshly cut balsam, spruce, and pine. Rooms piled with evergreens fill the house with their youth, pungent sap trumpeting the far-off spring when once again green will conquer a drab countryside.

A wrinkled woman, bent with age, welcomes us at the door. After greeting us with a smile, she proudly inclines her head to the man behind her.

"My husband," she beams, withdrawing to a nearby room where we can watch her weaving greens she has gathered from the cold with stiff fingers.

Rushing water, aromatic balsam are now overridden by the blazing personality before us, ensconced in a Rube Goldberg contraption. Can a cup be more than full? Can one be more than completely joyous? Our host, with scanty white hair and a face as young as a baby's, engages us in animated conversation, as though our arrival were the most significant event of his life. Age, poverty, the fact that he is paraplegic only seem to make the fire in his bright eyes burn brighter, obliterating the cold and dark we know lurk just outside the door.

Lilies border the "icon" of this house and its occupants, their pure perfume mingling with the evergreens. Centered in the top of the frame is a crucifix. Before it we humble ourselves and kneel, refusing to "cloud the truth with ill-considered words." We didn't design the picture, nor can we go beyond the frame to see it in context.

Faith is the way we penetrate the blackness outside,

the way we transcend temporal hardship. But what endures is so unspeakably marvelous that evil is insignificant by comparison. "Eye has not seen nor ear heard . . ." (1 Corinthians 2:9).

Nones

Ninth Hour

"Blessed is the Kingdom of the Father and of the Son and of the Holy Spirit . . ."

DIVINE LITURGY OF ST. JOHN CHRYSOSTOM

By the time we reach Nones, the harsh glare of midday has been muted, Sext's intensity maturing into something softer: the deepening glow of late afternoon when sun manifests its full triumph. We're given a glimpse of the peaceable kingdom during the afternoon sun's reign before it slides down the western sky to sleep behind the horizon. Travelers begin to think of where they'll spend the night; people at work turn their thoughts toward home.

If Nones were a month, it would be August. Wheat tassels scintillate the fields; sun-ripened grapes begin to blush. Bursting with berries, fields ripe for the harvest, her roadsides garnished with magenta liatris and golden-rod, August gleams, gilded by a whole summer of sun. Toward day's end, images of home also acquire a warm glow, burnished by accumulated memories of family and friends around the table sharing food, laughing at stories, delighted by children.

The homeward journey: if we're prayer, we're on it. Yet some of us, like two disciples walking toward Emmaus late in the afternoon of the Resurrection, have no idea who is walking beside us or what home beckons.

> So they drew near to the village to which they were going. He acted as if He were going farther, but they urged Him strongly, saying, "Stay with us, for it is toward evening, and the day is now far spent." So He went in to stay with them. When He was at table with them, He took the bread, blessed and broke it, and gave it to them. And their eyes were opened: they recognized Him. Then He vanished from their sight. They said to each other, "Did not our hearts burn within us while He spoke to us on the road, when He explained the scriptures to us?"
>
> (LUKE 24:28–32)

When Christ blessed and broke the bread that evening, the disciples recalled His last meal with them, "and their eyes were opened." They recognized Him, saw that He was risen, and, as He explained Scripture to them, understood that *He* was its meaning.

Then they realized that the home toward which they had been walking was the Kingdom of God. Rather than being obliterated by Golgotha, as they had feared, the Kingdom was only truly established in the aftermath of the death of their earthly hopes.

The disciples understood Christ's invitation when He handed each a piece of bread. On the evening He was betrayed, breaking bread, He had said, "This is My body, which is given for you." Since Friday's catastrophe every one of Christ's followers knew what "given for you" meant in all its horrible particularity. Now He was inviting them to share the life of that body, no longer of this world, but risen.

Scripture speaks of "the fullness of time." Nones is the fullness of day. By its ripened light, more mature because of the hour that precedes it, we are able to see prayer in its fullest expression: the Eucharist, gathering all the fragments of our individual lives to offer them as part of the whole grateful hymn of redeemed creation.

Early in the history of the chosen people, the Israelites understood the Lord to be the source of every good they enjoyed. He had blessed them, and they returned thanks by offering Him their first fruits. Our Eucharist (from the Greek *eucharistia,* meaning "thanksgiving") is the fullness of giving back, of "blessing" God, of saying "thank you." For we are able to offer the One "through whom all things were made," returning the entire cosmos, transformed in Him, to the Father.

The divine Alchemist, the Holy Spirit, breathing over the waters at creation, inseparable from the Word of the Father, transmutes the dreadful deadly scene of the Crucifixion into one of unspeakable joy and inextinguishable life. Christ died in truth and, as He did so, exposed every sadistic, degrading, nasty aspect of fallen human nature exhibited by those who betrayed and put Him to death. He drank the bitter cup of abandonment, of utter loneliness, to the dregs while hanging above those He had come to deliver—whose response was to jeer at His agonizing death.

We who are fortunate enough to view Sext bathed in the golden afterglow of Nones see beyond the ugly reality of Christ's death. Contrary to appearances, what happened was that the world died when it rejected Jesus.

He is unquenchable life—and the world refused (as it still refuses) its own true life when it killed Him.[23]

But when Jesus died, He died only to the world's corpse: to fragmented time, to sin, to all darkness incompatible with light. When, by the power of the Holy Spirit, He rose, He "trampled down death by death," as we sing at Pascha. The life in Him, more powerful than all the forces a dead world could array against Him, blazed forth through the Holy Spirit from the Resurrection to Pentecost, and from Pentecost through all the centuries of the Gathering to the present.

Are we in the twenty-first century, so distant from these events, left with mere words and triumphant otherworldly images? No. In fact, Resurrection iconography is not at all triumphant. Neither is it otherworldly. In the most common Resurrection icon we see a glorified Christ bending with infinite compassion to lift Adam and Eve (us) out of the dark half-life of their longing for Him.

Another icon depicts an angel in white sitting by the empty tomb, shroud and *souderian* on the floor nearby. A third shows us the bewildered myrrh-bearing women overcome by grief.

But images alone, helpful as they are, cannot feed faith for two thousand years. Manna sustained the

Israelites during their wanderings in the wilderness. Sustaining us with God's Word, flesh and blood, as we meander in contemporary wildernesses, the Eucharist is our manna.

At the Last Supper we were bequeathed the Eucharist: the new Passover meal, the liturgical re-presentation of Christ's gift of Himself to us. As we celebrate it in different times and places, with different people, we, with all that we touch in our lives, are drawn into Christ's priestly, transformative action, becoming part of it, becoming prayer—together.

Quietly, unnoticed by the world that has died, the healing action of Christ continues through His body, gathering together the elements of creation that are forming the Kingdom and offering the whole to God.

Shall we rerun the Paschal film to the Last Supper? Viewed from the warmth and joy of the Resurrection and freed of the shadow of Judas and the garden of Gethsemane, what elements lodge most securely in our memories? Christ's farewell words and two episodes.

At the end of Christ's final discourse He prays to His Father for the kind of unity among His followers that He and the Father enjoy.

> "I do not ask for these only, but also for those who will
> believe in Me through their word, that they all may be

> one just as You, Father, are in Me and I in You, that
> they also may be in Us so that the world may believe
> that You have sent Me."
>
> (JOHN 17:20–21)

He further elaborates this thought in such a way as to make it perfectly clear how essential unity is if we are to express and build the Kingdom and attract others to it. Unity is not optional; it's a sign of the Church that is one, holy, catholic (meaning all-inclusive, not limited to national or ethnic groups), and apostolic.

Shame on every Christian denomination for its departures from this profound prayer uttered just before Christ's betrayal, passion, and death. We all, all denominations, are guilty to some extent, and we all need a change of heart. What witnesses might we be if we behaved more like Christ, seeking to emphasize what we share in Him rather than revealing our lack of humility, our fearful clinging to ethnic, sectarian cliques, to things that don't matter as we ignore those that do.

The simple fact is that our disunity reflects our distance from Christ. All we need for Christianity to be one is for the faithful in all denominations to draw closer to Him, and to expend the necessary energy to remove the "logs" obstructing our vision.

The Last Supper's first episode, Christ washing the

feet of His disciples, is an icon of humility and a meta-phor for Christ's putting aside His divinity in order to become one of us.

> "Do you understand what I have done to you? You call me 'Teacher' and 'Lord,' and you are right, for so I am. If I then, your Lord and teacher, have washed your feet, you also ought to wash one another's feet."
>
> (JOHN 13:12–15)

This is a variation on the great commandment, with Christ claiming the place of God and describing love of neighbor as humble service. Humility, bowing in reverent service before the other, whether God or man, is the key to the Kingdom and an essential mark of the true pray-er.

> Have these sentiments in you which are in Christ Jesus, who, although divine, did not cling to the state of equality with God, but emptied Himself, assuming the condition of a servant: becoming human and behaving as a man.
>
> (PHILIPPIANS 2:5–7)

> "Truly I say to you: unless you turn about and become again like children, you will not enter the Kingdom of Heaven."
>
> (MATTHEW 18:3)

Humility in Jesus is quite another thing from the virtue required of us. To share our humanity, to enter creation as a man, He had to bend low, veiling His divinity, hiding the full truth of who He was to win us from within the limitations of our nature.

Nor is this all. He patterns humility for us, especially by washing the feet of the disciples. There is no other reason for the action. But even this is not enough. He suffers with us, not just the ordinary indignities or hurts of earthly life, but the most severe torturing, shameful, humiliating death, the death of the cross.

The measure of God's love, although it is without measure, can be glimpsed using the yardstick of Christ's humility. And this measurement of the immeasurable applies also to our value in God's eyes, as well as to the wonders of the life in Him for which we were created. Like children we ask God how much He loves us, and He replies from the Cross, "This much . . ."

Jesus' humility is the antidote to Adam's arrogance. If humility is only the partial truth of who He is, it is the complete truth of who we are. Humility recognizes the truth of the human nature He has condescended to share with us: created human nature which we have distorted by sin. If we begin to grasp what this means, we understand why, without humility, there is no truth or life in us. And we'll also realize why humility unlocks the gate of the Kingdom. Without it, *metanoia* is impossible; faith is impossible; love is impossible.

The blessing of bread and cup with words that changed their significance for all time is the second episode. This is Christ's last will and testament, meant to be executed in the context of a Paschal meal. It's unlikely that the Last Supper was actually the Passover meal. What is clear, though, is that the events of Holy Week happened in the *context* of Passover: at that time and with reference to it.

"Do this," He said, "in memory of Me" (Luke 22:19), deliberately echoing God's words to the Jews of the Exodus: "This day [Passover] shall be for you a memorial day, and you shall keep it as a feast to the Lord, throughout your generations, as a statute forever, you shall keep it as a feast" (Exodus 12:14).

"Remember," God commanded the Jews, and He gave them the way to *do* that remembrance. "Do this in memory of Me," Jesus commanded His followers, who would later recall His words to the crowd at Capernaum. In that discourse, after declaring that He was the reality of which the manna in the desert was a sign, Jesus went further:

"I am the bread of life. Your fathers ate manna in the wilderness, and they died. This is the bread that comes down from heaven so that one may eat of it and not die. I am the living bread that came down from heaven. If anyone eats of this bread, he will live forever. And the bread that I will give for the life of the world is My flesh."

(JOHN 6:48–51)

After this discourse, which, in full, could not be more explicit, many of His disciples went away. Jesus turned to the twelve apostles. "Do you want to go away as well?" Impulsive Peter answers for every person of faith: "Lord, to whom shall we go? You have the words of everlasting life."

Nones represents the generative aspect of prayer, which, like the Paschal mystery, initiates, expands, and gives fullness of life to what precedes and follows it. What appears to be conflict—the opposing vertical and horizontal lines of the cross, human versus divine, all that goes against our inclinations—is actually what gives life.

In our own development, obstacles or apparent contradictions that cause us to suffer and reflect are catalysts for growth as no steady, unconflicted state can be. Nones reconciles all the generative elements at the banquet of the Word, tasted in Scripture and Holy Communion. But before returning to the Eucharist, let's pause a moment to reflect on memory, so essential to any consideration of Eucharist.

God indicated the importance of remembering when He commanded the Jews to remember the Passover each year, anchoring remembrance in specific actions and words. He knew, as they would come to know, that their corporate act of remembrance would constitute and keep them as a people.[24]

At the Last Supper, Christ's "Do this in memory of Me" restates the Passover command. After Pentecost, the apostles recalled Christ's blessing of the bread and wine at the Last Supper, understanding them anew in the light of the Holy Spirit they had just received.

As the Seder Supper, renewed in every faithful Jewish home at Passover, unites each Jewish family with others throughout time and space, the re-presentation of the Lord's Supper does the same for the People of God of the new dispensation. Seder and Eucharist share certain symbolism, while differing as shadow differs from reality or prophecy from fulfillment.

Memory is not simply a bin for storing moments of experience. Memory is that aspect of our interior being that "gathers up the fragments." Through it we sew our life together, making sense of it so that the whole is greater than the sum of its parts. Just as time is something other than our measurement of it, shrinking and expanding in ways that do not correspond to hours, minutes, and seconds, memory far transcends simple recall of past events.

Book X of St. Augustine's *Confessions* is an exploration of memory that can deepen our own perception of it and help us to see it from perspectives we may not have considered before.[25]

Why is this important? Because remembering is the quintessential act of a person, a profound activity emanating from the heart, where the image of God in us is being either polished or defaced. Through memory, we hold past and future events in being in a way analogous to God's holding all creation in existence. It's a subject infinitely more important than the attention it has received to date suggests.

Our capacity to remember is thrown into relief by elements of modernity that threaten it. Television—with its scattershot bits of advertisements, its rapid-fire episodic presentations that aid and abet, if not create, short attention spans—devastates memory.

Overexposure to news presented in short meaningless blurts saturates the mind with info-litter, impeding memory's proper function. Assaulted by sound bytes, our minds lose some of their ability to prioritize, to weight things properly in relation to what matters in life, to see emerging patterns.

The Church sings "Eternal Memory" when one of us dies, not as a pious wish that people will remember us forever (they won't!), but as a prayer that God will, and that the essence of us—that which holds our moments together, our memory—will remain forever.

Memory is our heart operating on our experience. It's that function in us that digests and sorts what we take in from the world in which we live. By means of it we are able to project our minds into the future. For our ability to forge a future depends on ingredients already within us, depends on memory (even when the forging is a departure from those ingredients). Here, in memory, in our hearts, resides our priesthood: here we gather up our part of existence to offer it in union with the cosmic offering of Christ to our Father.

Which brings us again to Eucharist and the Holy Anaphora. *Anaphora* is a Greek rhetorical term derived from a word meaning "carrying back," in the sense that a word repeated in several successive phrases "remembers" its previous expressions.

In the Divine Liturgy, the Holy Anaphora is the offering of the bread and wine and their transmutation into Christ by the power of the Holy Spirit, "carrying us back" to Christ's passion, death, and resurrection. It is the *memoria* of the Divine Liturgy. It is Passover fulfilled, Christ's Paschal offering re-presented, and our conscious participation in it. Every repetition of it gathers up all the others, digesting them anew in Christ.

Father Alexander Schmemann tells us in *For the Life of the World*:

> In the Bible the food that man eats, the world of which He must partake in order to live, is given to him by God, and is given as *communion with God.* The world as man's food is not something "material" and limited to material functions, thus different from, and opposed to, the specifically "spiritual" functions by which man is related to God. All that exists is God's gift to man, and it all exists to make God known to man, to make man's life communion with God. It is divine love made food, made life for man. God blesses everything He creates, and, in biblical language, this means that He makes all creation the sign and means of His presence and wisdom, love and revelation: "O taste and see that the Lord is good."[26]

Now do we begin to understand life as a feast? Do the parables of the Kingdom of God as a banquet take on new meaning? If so, a triptych for Nones will come as no surprise.

Its central image is of the apostles, in classical draped garments, reclining at table with their Lord. He is in the act of sharing the cup:

"Drink of it, all of you, for this is My blood of the covenant which is poured out for many for the forgiveness of sins. I tell you I will not drink of this fruit of the vine until that day when I drink of it new with you in My Father's kingdom."

(MATTHEW 26:27–29)

Unlike the Lauds icon, this one does not stun us with brilliant, clear light. Its colors are those of Nones: deep, warm, and inviting. Christ's gaze is still that of the Pantokrator of Sinai, but we are now included in the picture, represented by apostles whose expressions range from thoughtful wonder to bewildered incomprehension. All the faces profess profound attention and love for their Lord.

To the left of the Last Supper is a vividly executed painting of the first Passover meal. An Israelite family stands within a house whose lintels have been marked with the blood of the roasted lamb they are hastily consuming with bitter herbs. They are dressed for travel, staffs in hand. Above them in the night sky, an angel is suspended with uplifted hands, as if sparing this household the disaster he metes out to every Egyptian home.

A contemporary video contained in the frame on the right combines movement and sound with images. The tropical trees, colorful costumes, and dark skins of the people telegraph that we are in Africa as surely as does hearing drums in the jungle. Kenyans, their emaciated faces made beautiful by faith tried in the fire of persecution, sing the Divine Liturgy in a partially built church. They are clearly visible because the walls are only four feet high. A group of healthy young Americans with a priest and his family have come to assist the Kenyans in building this church to replace one obliterated by terrorists who murdered many of them and destroyed nearly everything capable of sustaining the lives of the survivors. As one absorbs the unearthly beauty of these people and hears familiar Greek melodies and words sung as only Africans can sing them, it is clear that the

Americans who came to help received much more than they gave.

Just as predictable as the central icon, the framing combines a vine twining about all three images, with here and there a cluster of ripe purple grapes. Interwoven with the vine are stalks of golden wheat. At the peak of the central icon is a round loaf of bread, and sloping toward it on either side are the words, "One Bread" and "One Body."

Gathering together to worship Father, Son, and Holy Spirit by re-presenting Christ's Passover is the work of the Church. It's what makes us Church. Incorporated into Christ at baptism, we fulfill the priestly life we have received and build the Kingdom when we participate in the Eucharist. "Thy Kingdom come," we pray. "Thy Kingdom come" we *do* when our hearts receive the world God gives us as a gift of His love and offer it back to Him as our love transformed in Christ. The process of perceiving the gifts we are given as God's love, of taking them into ourselves and allowing them, through the Holy Spirit within us, to divinize us is what happens to us individually in true prayer: theosis, divinization.

For the duration of the liturgy it is as though we have

been swept into the eternal present, into the Kingdom of God. The entire eucharistic prayer mimics our theosis as litanies wash over us like waves of repeated petition and we enter more and more deeply into Christ's priestly action: transmuting world-for-itself back into world-for-God.

The Eucharist draws individual "pray-ers," with all the *milieux* being transformed through them, together into the Holy Anaphora of Christ. There the whole body of Christ consciously offers all creation, "digested" in the Holy Spirit, to the Father.

Prayer takes place in our hearts, transforms them so that they become expressions of love of God and one another. Prayer at the heart, the *memoria*, of the Church is the Holy Anaphora, which expresses and fulfills itself in an eruption of mutual joy: Holy Communion.

In the first part of the Divine Liturgy God feeds us with His Word in Scripture. Having taken the Word into our hearts, we prepare ourselves for the Holy Anaphora by singing the Cherubic Hymn and by bringing forward the Holy Gifts in the Great Entrance. Settings of this hymn express the profound seriousness, the incomprehensibly exalted nature of what is to follow, plunging us into a depth of corporate prayer that is startling. At the end of it we pray that we may "put aside all earthly cares so that we may receive into ourselves the King of all."

Nothing magic occurs when the priest utters the words of Christ at the Last Supper over the bread and wine. It is the remembering, the Holy Anaphora. After Christ's words over the bread and wine, the priest prays quietly:

> Remembering, therefore, this saving commandment and all that came to pass for our sake—the Cross, the tomb, the resurrection on the third day, the ascension into heaven, the enthronement at the right hand, the second and glorious coming . . .

The priest then offers the gifts "from Your own gifts" aloud. The congregation either kneels or bows deeply for the invocation to the Holy Spirit. The priest asks God to "send down Your Holy Spirit upon us and upon these gifts here offered." As he continues to pray, the people concur repeatedly by their "amens."

Here, in the hearts of priest and people, is the locus of the action of the Holy Spirit that transforms the Holy Gifts. Something profoundly mysterious happens during the liturgy, and especially at the *epiclesis*, when we, the Gathering, pray with all the focused concentration of our hearts: Christ is made truly present in the Holy Spirit.

The dramatic movement, having reached its turning point in the Holy Anaphora and the epiclesis, is fulfilled in the banquet. Together we, who have reaffirmed the faith we share by reciting the symbol of it, the Creed, prepare to receive its reality. Together, we, having offered the world back to the Father in love and thanksgiving, pray the prayer Christ taught us. Having readied our hearts, we approach the table with humble awe to receive our offering, now transformed into Christ, as nourishment unto life everlasting. In Holy Communion we dwell in world-for-God, meeting one another at the table, receiving a foretaste of the Kingdom that is not of this world.

"Seek first the Kingdom of God and His wholeness, and all these things will be added to you." When we first begin to seek God, the relinquishing of the "world," our own self-will, may feel like loss, but the truth is that the "cross" is the only way to truly know and enjoy the world. And, in the measure that we give, God gives back to us: "Good measure, pressed down, shaken together, running over will be put into your lap" (Luke 6:38).

When I first came to St. Nicholas Church in St. Louis, I was struck by the symbolism of the center aisle. During the Divine Liturgy it was only used for the Little Entrance with the Gospel book and for the Great Entrance with the eucharistic gifts, until the time came for Holy Communion.

Then the aisle became a great road with throngs of reverent people joyfully pouring out of the pews, old and young, parents with babies in their arms or holding small children by the hand. It was like a mystical combination of the Yellow Brick Road with the Great Trunk Road of India transmuted into the highway to the Kingdom.

A much smaller church, St. Jacob of Alaska in North-field, Vermont, preserves other beautiful images, closer in time to the present. Its tininess seems to imprint the countenance of each communicant vividly on one's heart. Joy bounces like light from faces as each leaves the cup for the table with the *antidoron* (the unconsecrated bread broken from the loaf to be offered). The woman ahead of me receives Holy Communion, then turns around, sweeping the ground with her fingers as she bows deeply. Although surprised, I know her and what she means. She has just received Christ and is bowing to one who is about to receive Him.

A man, having noticed a stranger, crosses the nave to offer him the antidoron. The mutual embrace we enjoy at Communion includes even those who cannot partake of it fully. "Blessed is the Kingdom of the Father and of the Son and of the Holy Spirit, now and always, unto ages of ages." As we draw our experience of this Kingdom down into our hearts we can understand it more fully by recalling Christ's words about it.

"The Kingdom of Heaven is like treasure hidden in a field which a man found and covered up. Then in his joy he goes and sells all that he has and buys that field."

(MATTHEW 13:44)

"Again, the Kingdom of Heaven is like a net that was thrown into the sea and gathered fish of every kind. When it was full, men drew it ashore and sat down and sorted the good into containers, but threw away the bad."

(MATTHEW 13:47–50)

"To what shall I compare the Kingdom of God? It is like leaven that a woman took and hid in three measures of flour until it was all leavened."

(LUKE 13:20–21)

Incapable of being captured in a single concept, the Kingdom of heaven is a mystery never completely grasped by our finite minds, yet capable of being experienced.

And we can penetrate the mystery by living according to Christ's precepts, receiving His healing touch in the sacraments, assimilating His words about it.

What Christ has said is that the Kingdom is within us and near; yet He also speaks of it as something toward which we are moving, something not yet fully accomplished. He compares its action to that of the mustard seed, developing from the tiniest of seeds into a tree, and to leaven, unobtrusively affecting flour, to which it has been added, until the whole is risen.

The Kingdom is invisibly at work until the end of time, when there will be ultimate clarification. A separation will occur between good and bad "fish," the latter being discarded. The "weeds" in God's garden will be pulled, leaving only what He planted.

All that occurs in time is for the Kingdom of God and its inhabitants. All suffering, all temporal evil is tolerated so that creatures who accept God's invitation to share His life may do so. We cannot see the whole in order to validate these statements, but we can trust the word of the One who gives us such assurances, and we can trust the evidence of our own experience.

For the life of God within us, the Holy Spirit, is its own validation. Our truest confirmation is experiencing the Kingdom of God in this life. In fact, if we do not experience it now, we won't be able to in the life to come.

Like late afternoon, Nones savors the fullness of the day coming to an end and looks toward the warmth of a shared meal with those we love. Its richly colored images seem to sing, "Oh, taste and see that the Lord is good," in every language known to man.

VESPERS

O joyous radiance! Pure brightness of the immortal Father, celestial and holy, blessed Jesus Christ! Having come to the setting of the sun we behold the light of evening and hymn Father, Son, and Holy Spirit. Because You are worthy to be praised at all times with joyously singing voices, O life-giving Son of God, all the earth sings praises to You.

PHOS HILARON, *O GLADSOME LIGHT*

The hour of Vespers—peaceful, deep, sonorous—arrives with a medley of images like inflamed colors left in the wake of a fiery sun's plunge into the west. Bells toll for evensong; a gondola glides through the canals of Venice, parting images of flying storks on the mirrored surface of the water with its rippling ribbons of sunset color.

Echoes of the Barcarolle from Offenbach's *The Tales of Hoffman* sway through a mind susceptible to this quiet time and season of the prayerful heart. This is an hour for reflection when our boat, having busied itself about many things during the day, sails quietly into its harbor to tie up for the night.

> It is good to give thanks to the Lord,
> Singing praises to Your name, O Most High;
> Declaring Your love at daybreak
> And Your faithfulness all through the night
> To melodies of ten-stringed lyre and zither,
> And a soft murmur of harp.
> For You, O Lord, have delighted me by Your deeds;
> Before all You have made, I sing for joy.
> How great are Your works, O Lord!
> How unfathomable Your thoughts!
> The stupid man cannot know,
> Nor can the fool understand this:
> That though the wicked sprout like grass
> And all evildoers flourish,
> They are doomed to destruction forever.
> But You, O Lord, remain exalted forever.
> For behold, Your enemies, O Lord:
> Your enemies perish,
> And all evildoers are scattered!
> (PSALM 92:1–9)

Possibly the best known of the Church's hours, Vespers is the evening prayer of both Eastern and Western churches, a faint echo of the Jewish evening lamp-lighting service. From Genesis 1:5, "And there was evening and morning: the first day," and the Jewish understanding that a day extended from one sunset to another, Christians derived the custom of beginning the celebration of the Lord's day and other feasts the evening before.

In the writings of St John Cassian, this evening service was known as the *Vespertina Synaxis* or *Vespertina Solemnitas*. Also known as *Lucernaria Hora* or *Lucernalis* (candle-lighting time), its characteristic hymn, *Phos Hilaron,* was already ancient in the fifth century.

Just as Lauds (Matins in the East) is the great morning prayer, Vespers is its evening counterpart. And, just as some historical-structural confusion attends Lauds-Matins, there is analogous confusion attending Vespers. Put simply, the Church intends the Magnificat (or, in the East, a Theotokion) and the Canticle of Simeon to be among the final prayers of the day. Since Vespers is the last liturgical hour for most, these prayers are included in it although they are also part of Compline. To avoid repetition they will be included only in our Compline, since it is the last of our hours. Suffice it to say that Vespers shares some of Compline's qualities.

If, as we did with Nones, we choose a month to describe it, October seems appropriate for Vespers. For in the same way that the sun summons all the rich tints of the day through which it has traveled to make a final coloratura display before it sinks behind the hills, the waning year gathers its forces into a last explosion of brilliant October color before going dormant.

Vespers sums up and, with lavish splendor, distills our day, reminding us of the "joyous radiance": Christ, the "glorious outpouring of the immortal Father." At the same time, it introduces us to the luminosity of that clear pale evening light that follows sunset and whose transparency, like the glassy light of October, hints at what lies behind and beyond. Vespers celebrates the radiant beauty of the whole, the *Phos Hilaron*, Christ, through whom we view both cosmos and Creator.

Teetering between day and night, between this world and the next, we watch the sun disappear. And, like the apostles at the Ascension when the true Sun was removed from their sight, we stand awestruck, gazing up to heaven. We hear the crystalline voices of angels: "Men of Galilee, why do you stand looking up at the sky? This Jesus, who was taken up from you into the heavens, will come in the same way as you saw Him go into the heavens" (Acts 1:11).

Remembering and holding the sunset vision in our inmost hearts, we return our gaze to the world in which we still live. After our day illumined by Christ, we perceive that world with more clarity and more truth. Like stones washed by the River Una, everything has intensified.

Psalm 104, the great Vespers psalm, returns our life-in-the-world to us, the one we have offered to the Father, now washed in the Spirit so that we see it afresh with its every vibrant detail.

Bless the Lord, O my soul!
O Lord my God, what magnificence is Yours,
Clothed in majesty and glory,
Robed in swirls of light!
You spread the heavens like a tent.
Above the rains You build Your dwelling.
You make Your chariot of clouds,
And on the wings of the wind You come and go.
You make winds Your messengers;
Flames of fire, Your attendants.
You settled the earth on its foundation,
Unshakeable from age to age.
Once deep ocean covered it like a cloak:
Its waters stood higher than the mountains.

At Your rebuke they took flight,
Fleeing at the clap of Your thunder,
Leaving mountain heights to rise,
Valleys to sink into their appointed places.
And to these waters You set frontiers they might not pass
Lest they flow back to cover earth again.
Yet springs still gush forth in the glens:
Flowing among the hills,
Giving drink to all beasts of the field.
Here wild donkeys quench their thirst,
While above riverbanks roost the birds of heaven
Leafing the boughs with their musical notes.
From Your dwelling on high You water the hills;
Earth drinks her fill from Your hand,
Growing grass for cattle.
For man, too, she puts forth green plants
That he may draw wheat from her bosom
And wine to gladden his heart.
Then oil will make his face shine
And bread will strengthen his heart.
The trees of the Lord are full of sap,
Cedars He planted on the Lebanon
Where sparrows nestle.
The stork lodges atop junipers,
Goats among high mountains,
And badgers burrow among the rocks.
You made the moon to mark the seasons;
The sun, who knows when it is time for bed.
When You spread darkness, night falls;
Creatures creep forth, and the forest begins to stir.

Young lions roar after their prey,
Clamoring to God for their food.
At sunrise they slink away to lie down in their lairs
As man goes abroad to toil until evening falls.
How manifold are Your works, O Lord!
What wisdom designed them!
All the earth is filled with Your creatures:
The ocean, wide and vast,
Teeming with countless swarms
Of living things both large and small.
Ships glide by them as does Leviathan,
Whom You created to make Yourself laugh.
The eyes of all look hopefully to You, O Lord,
To give them their food in due season.
You provide, they gather. You open Your hand
And fill every living creature with good things.
You hide Your face and they cringe.
You take back Your Spirit, they breathe no more,
Returning to the dust from which they came.
You send forth Your Spirit; they are created afresh,
And You renew the face of the earth.
May the glory of the Lord endure forever!
May the Lord ever delight in His creatures!
A glance from Him and earth trembles;
A touch and mountains belch smoke.
I will sing to the Lord as long as I live,
Make music for Him while I have breath.
May my meditation be pleasing to Him
In whom all my joy rests.
May sinners vanish from the earth

And the impious be no more.
Bless the Lord, O my soul!

By the time we reach Vespers, we may have noticed that our journey is both circular and progressive. We are moving toward an endpoint, from alpha toward omega, yet our forward progression is accomplished by spiraling inward to the present. The sun set yesterday, but we've not arrived at that *same* sunset. Today's is analogous, not identical, to yesterday's.

The church day really begins on its eve with Vespers, developing the Jewish understanding from Genesis most perceptible in the celebration of the Sabbath, which begins on Friday evening. That same devout mood experienced in the lighting of candles and the prayerful blessing recited in Jewish families is carried forward to Christian Vespers.

With the setting of the sun on Saturday, Great Vespers initiates the "eighth day" in which creation lives after the Resurrection. It's a heavenly beginning, a new creation that starts the day after the Sabbath. For the Sabbath, though still revered, now belongs to the old dispensation; Easter has left it behind. Now we celebrate the Lord's Day, Sunday.

The eighth day, added after the seven of the first

Creation, embraces all time until it is fulfilled in the Second Coming. It reminds us that already we have begun to "live and move and have our being" consciously in the Kingdom of the Father, Son, and Holy Spirit. All is now interpenetrated with the breath of the Holy Spirit, with prayer.

Contemplative prayer—reflective, interior, bathing what we do in what we have become in Christ—is the essence of Vespers. In a sense, it's the afterglow of Nones. What happens in the Divine Liturgy—the offering, its transformation into Christ and communion—doesn't remain in the church building, but travels in us out into the world—this world we are to leaven and flavor with the abundant life acquired during the "work," the *leitourgeia*, that is the Church's service to the world.

Vespers' translucent quality may be illustrated by a story from Father Peter Knowles, O.P.:

> Once, when spending some days at the monastery of Sihastrea in Moldavia, I was farewelled by the Superior (Higumen) whom I had not seen during my time in the monastery. He came to the door and apologised for his absence, wished me well and said "I have been some days working out in the monastery's forest. That was my Liturgy for this period." A living example of what Abbot Aemilianos of Simonas Petras [on Mt.

Athos] has written: "Each monk, in serving the needs of his own brethren, is performing the Liturgy of the one body and giving an account of himself as a faithful steward."[27]

By the luminous light of evening, we may now be able to see the day with *all* its work as part of the Divine Liturgy. And by that same light we may see our own personal work with new clarity. We are to pray always. Since work is a necessity for our survival, then it too must become prayer. How?

Whatever way our talents, inclinations, and circumstances converge in the work we do is capable of being worship if it's true to who and what we are being called to become. By the gentle lamplight of Vespers we consider our work and how it relates to our real destiny. After reflection we may choose to question either the work itself or the way we do it.

"Thy Kingdom come . . ." Does the work I perform help to build the Kingdom? Are my relations with others expressive of the love of God in my heart? Is my life and the work I do to sustain it iconic of the Kingdom of God? Is the Kingdom "the one thing necessary," the "pearl of great price," or merely a nice abstraction to which I assent?

"What is man that You are mindful of him?" asks the

psalmist. We who dwell in the "eighth day," who have died with Christ in baptism and are rising with Him through the Holy Spirit, know from the sacrifice of the cross how dear man is to the heart of God. For man is the heart, the *memoria*, of God's creation. We, body, soul, and spirit, participate in all aspects of creation and, in Christ, are able to draw the parts we touch into the Kingdom through the metamorphosis occurring in our own hearts as they digest the world.

> O Lord, our Lord, how majestic is Your name in all the
>   earth!
> You have set Your glory above the heavens.
> From the mouths of babes and infants comes praise
>   of You,
> Confounding Your adversaries,
> Silencing the malicious and the vengeful.
> When I look at Your heavens, the work of Your fingers,
> The moon and the stars which You have set in place,
> What is mortal man that You are mindful of him,
> Adam's offspring, that You wish to visit him?
> Yet You have made him little less than divine,
> Crowning him with glory and honor.
> You have given him dominion over the work of Your
>   hands,
> Putting all things under his feet:
> All sheep and oxen and even the wild animals,
> The birds in the sky and the fish in the sea,

When he travels the paths of the seas.
O Lord, our Lord, how majestic is Your name in all
    the earth!
(PSALM 8)

Vespers is not only sunset but is also the time for lighting lamps and candles. We were not bereft of all light when the sun set but have been given fire to illuminate the dark.

Candles, now usually associated with prayer in church, have a place in private prayer too. Simply lighting a candle has an intrinsic holiness about it of light shining in darkness, life asserting itself against death. Somehow prayer is assisted by the flickering, living flames of candles, symbolic of angelic presences and of the spirit within us. No more explicable than the mysterious holiness of water, the presence of lit candles exerts an influence over our prayer.

The difference between walking into an unlit church and being welcomed by the warmth and beauty of lighted candles is analogous to the contrast between coming to a dinner table that is unset and unlit and the welcome we feel when everything is prepared and candles are shining.

In a conversation with Father Mark Sherman, OCA, he revealed his own strong conviction on this point by saying that the first thing he does when he goes into the church is to light candles. Even if no liturgy is to follow, this means that anyone who happens by, seeing the open door, enters a living, welcoming, lighted church.

Sir John Betjeman captures something of the blessing that is church candlelight in a poem he wrote after visiting in Greece:

The domed interior swallows up the day.
Here, where to light a candle is to pray,
The candle flame shows up the almond eyes
Of local saints who view with no surprise
Their martyrdoms depicted upon walls
On which the filtered daylight faintly falls.
The flame shows up the cracked paint—sea-green
    blue
And red and gold, with grained wood showing
    through–
Of much kissed ikons, dating from, perhaps,
The fourteenth century. There across the apse,
Ikon and oleograph-adorned is seen
The semblance of an English chancel screen.
'With oleographs?' you say. 'Oh what a pity!
Surely the diocese has some committee
Advising it on taste?' It is not so.
Thus vigorously does the old tree grow,
By persecution pruned, watered with blood,
Its living roots deep in pre-Christian mud.

> It needs no bureaucratical protection.
> It is its own perpetual resurrection.[28]

Others have noted that we in the West may worship God's goodness and truth but sometimes overlook His beauty. Candles are part of our acknowledgment of God's beauty as well as our humble attempt to mimic it.

Incense and bells resemble candles by also celebrating a beauty suggestive of invisible realities. Like the candle flame, incense rises, perfuming the space around icons and worshipers. Each time we are censed during the Divine Liturgy, a profound wave of consciousness of the holy washes over us, drawing us deeper and deeper into the mystery we are celebrating.

Bells may or may not play a role in our private prayer, but they, too, are important sanctifiers of physical space. While candles appeal to our senses of sight, smell, and touch, and incense to sight and smell, bells address our ears.

Ancients imagined the air around them crowded with spirits who would flee before vibrations set in motion by the ringing of bells. Even today there are times when a priest is preceded by a bell-ringer, not so much to chase away evil spirits as to signify and prepare us for the approach of the holy.

And for centuries the sound of church bells summoning the faithful or remembering the Incarnation through the Angelus has been an integral part of the beauty of many cities, towns, and villages. Joyful jingling bells accompany liturgical censings, especially in Orthodoxy, where twelve small bells are attached to the chains of the censer. Representing the apostles, eleven of the bells make music; the twelfth, the Judas bell, is dumb.

Yet the helps we employ in prayer are not meant to make a division between two sorts of time: secular and sacred. Rather the heightened awareness they support reveals the essential sacredness of all time, hinting, through the senses we employ to perceive the world, at the holiness it veils.

> O You who willingly gave me Your flesh for food, You who are a fire to consume the unworthy, burn me not, my Creator, but actively enter into my joints, my inmost parts, strengthen both my brain and my bones and enlighten my five-fold senses.
>
> —COMMUNION PRAYER
> OF SIMEON METAPHRASTES (C. 960)

The free association of ideas that flood the mind at Vespers summons two memories. The first is of an event that took place after supper on Monhegan Island. A small group of vacationers strolled from the dining room to a west-facing rock overlooking the ocean, where they silently watched the sun's farewell to a gorgeous summer day. When the flamboyant display ended, the communal silence continued for the length of a deep breath, then broke into a spontaneous patter of applause.

* * * * * *

Twenty-nine years ago I found myself in Wilmington, North Carolina. On a wide thoroughfare a crumbling antebellum mansion sported a sign indicating it would take in guests for the night. I rang the doorbell. After a noticeable lapse of time it became apparent that a pair of eyes greatly magnified by Coke-bottle glasses was peering at me from the shadowy gloom beyond the screen door. I addressed them. "I'm looking for a place to stay the night."

The quavery old voice, embellished by its pronounced North Carolina accent, responded, "Do you have thirty dollahs?"

"I do." She looked unconvinced.

With increasing suspicion: "Wheah do you come from?" When I told her, she asked, with even more suspicion, "Wheah's yoah cah?" I pointed down the street, wondering whether she really intended the "Guests" sign or had absentmindedly left it hanging from another era.

Tentatively, she opened the door, and I entered a cavernous hall, its grand staircase of at least fifty steps edging up the wall before making a U-turn into the long gallery above us on the right. Enormous light fixtures, surely the first generation of such and remarkable for the quantity of their missing bulbs, dangled from the ceiling. A phalanx of buttons for the operation of these fixtures arrayed on a cluster of black wall plates failed to indicate their relationship to the ethereal chandeliers, and one wondered how the old lady could function by their light or manage to clamber up all those stairs.

After a brief conversation, my suitability as a lodger was ratified by precise directions to the room and the revelation of which one of the vast array of buttons could actually provoke light.

The room I was to occupy proved to be enormous, boasting five beds, an assortment of bureaus, dressing tables, and an old broken-down refrigerator plastered with onomatopoeic stickers like "Boom! Kafooey! Splat! Kerplunk!" A glance at the furnishings dispelled any lingering mystery about my hostess's effort to reassure me as I climbed the stairs:

"Patrishaaaa!" she'd called after me.

"Yes?"

"Don't you worry. Ah won't let anyone else in with you."

If the uncertain welcome hadn't indicated the precariousness of my position, the bathroom certainly did. Above an ancient marble basin hung a hand-lettered sign stating that failure to turn off a faucet or the light, or the commission of any of eight other felonies, "will result in termination of your stay."

Blissfully unaware that the neighborhood was renowned for its murders (two that very night), I wandered into the pellucid evening to find the restaurant recommended by my hostess, marveling at the fact that I was the sole pedestrian.

Fancy hangs an evening star against the lavender twilight because it belongs there. Memory isn't positive it was. My instructions propelled me down toward the Cape Fear River, where an image of its slumbering battleship remains the symbol of that sleepy old Southern city. The restaurant proved to be simply one large room full of tables occupied by happy, chattering groups of people. In a corner, the pianist, no more accomplished than I, played with all the panache of Liberace. Although alone, I felt included in the general bonhomie, savoring every bite of the delicious meal.

Visiting each table, beaming paternally on us all,

the genial owner of the establishment was the ground of our pleasure. As he wished each of us "good night" at the door, I realized that his was a great profession. Each evening he welcomed guests to the banquet of his day's labors and into his generous heart. He wasn't merely providing a meal or earning a living. He offered his guests a few hours of timeless enjoyment, of homeliness and love and happiness.

On the way back to my lodging, under a sky now verging on blue-black with a full moon, I was again the sole pedestrian with no cars at all on the streets. Coming up a hill, I was accosted by the splendor of a moonlit antebellum house in the throes of reconstruction. I had paused to admire it when a pair of eyes suspended in the darkness under what looked like a banana tree took me by surprise. They belonged to a black man, largely invisible under the circumstances, who apologized profusely for startling me.

Back in my room, I undressed and slipped between soft old sheets, savoring the experiences of the evening and the peculiarly warm quality of those sheets, their nostalgic scent summoning the entire human race, of which I felt myself a part in a new and more intimate way. Not even the fridge's noisy stickers prevented my falling into deep sleep, happy and peaceful as a child in loving arms.

The next morning I was preparing to take my leave after breakfast.

By then my hostess had narrated the salient details of her life. A retired teacher, she had inherited the house when a relative died. One needed little more than a glimpse through half-open pocket doors at her bedroom (once the dining room)—mountains of laundry, clusters of medicine bottles, and stacks of worn magazines—to fill in the rest of the story.

"Patrishaaaa," she appealed, "do you think you could stay on and keep me company? Do you have to go back to Chicago? I could really use some help, and we get on so well . . ."

I said I'd love to stay for a while, if my young son and work didn't prevent such a thing. "He could come too," she wheedled. My heart bled for her. This woman, whose thoughtful, intelligent mind waged a valiant battle each day with loneliness, age, and fear, deserved to be loved. And was.

For the last time, I mounted the stairs to collect my things, when the quavery voice floated up behind me. "Patrishaaa, before you leave would you mind just pulling up the sheets on your bed?"

In a flash I divined their indefinable human quality . . .

You may be wondering what this tale has to do with Vespers.

Only everything.

The sun sank behind Tiberias, and the last light was flung on the opposite hills. Every valley and crevice was clearly defined in the bright light. The clarity of the air made the opposite shores seem no more distant than a mile or so. The lake became a sheet of blue glass and no wind stirred the trees. Ripples widened on the still water where fish were jumping. Kingfishers flew like darts through the air. Gradually the last light of the sun grew from gold to brown on the hills. The valleys filled with blue shadows and a strange mauve color shimmered a moment and deepened into blue. The hills held the light of the vanished sun for a long time. The east glowed with a white incandescent radiance and a pink afterglow throbbed in the west. The silence was deep. The light splash of a fish, the clapping of pigeons in flight, and the scream of swifts were the only sounds. Far to the

north Mount Hermon lifted its wall of snow. All Nature seemed listening in the important hush of the sunset; and in this deep silence the first star burned above the Sea of Galilee.[29]

This beautiful image has a frame of twilight. There is a sound of lapping water and a quiet evening star at the top. The other three sides are simply the mildly luminous evening sky, each with one face suspended in it. On the left is the face of the black man, so concerned to have startled someone although he had done no more than stand quietly enjoying a lovely evening under a tree. On the right is the gregarious restaurateur, beaming affection to everyone he served, and, at the bottom, the countenance of my hostess revealing a heart more powerful than loneliness, ill health, and the fears of a helpless old lady.

> Let my prayer rise as incense before You;
> Let the lifting up of my hands be an evening sacrifice;
> Hear me, O Lord.
> (PSALM 141:2)

COMPLINE

Button of moon on a mantle of dark
Pinned to the blue sky by stars,
Sequins of silence piercing musical spheres
Singing inaudible light:
You are the truth of the cloak you adorn,
The truth of the mask we call night.

Nothing so deep as night. In darkness the familiar becomes strange. Who has not sensed mystery on a warm June evening twinkling with fireflies? Or, enveloped by velvet darkness, been oddly comforted by the steady zinging singing of cicadas? At midnight one August on an island in Maine, star-freckled heavens bent low above a freshly cut field, poetry so dizzying it confused symphonic stars with the incense of new-mown hay.

Stars shine on other summer nights, stars so fat one

can hardly believe they are only pinpricks of white in other skies . . . and moons: white, yellow, orange, fuzzy, cloud-draped, suspended like opalescent scimitars or circles of shine pasted on lapis. . . . All the heavenly bodies appear to us as piercings of the dark, outlets for the overwhelming light on the far side of night, visual whispers to comfort us when nature's other charms are shrouded.

We have come full circle. We're back in the dark time of the year, in the winter that returns as surely as spring, summer, and fall to season us; in the night from which we began our journey of the hours. Are we in the same place? Have all the fluting, mellow, silvery sounds the day produces made no difference to the bass notes with which we began?

One hopes they have illuminated the place and time of our origins—here and now—which are at once the gates of our germination and of our fruition, our *teleos*, our end. True prayer, hour by hour, season by season, always brings us deeper into *here* so we may penetrate *now* more profoundly. If Matins reminds us of creation, not as an action over and done with long ago, but as an ongoing process, we and all of creation are moving toward the fulfillment implicit in such beginning: Compline. The mystery of the seed containing the potential for what it will become is unfolded in Matins and fulfilled in Compline.

Science may describe the division of cells and the characteristic sequence of their journey from seed to mature organism. Yet behind all description and explanation lie a thousand "whys and wherefores" to which the only response is wonder.

What guides the seed, with no experience beyond itself as germ of life, along the twisty road to chestnut tree or zebra? Or shepherds us as we travel toward our own destiny? During this last hour, we cast an eye backward over the day to view our road from Matins night to Compline night.

When we arrive at the "darkness" produced by blinding light, "the point of intersection of the timeless with time," words elude us. We grasp at will-o'-the-wisps of language to describe this simple hour, when the only valid utterance is silence and a life become prayer. What follows is T. S. Eliot's effort in *Four Quartets* to grapple with the mystery of this moment:

> The point of intersection of the timeless
> With time, is an occupation for the saint—
> No occupation either, but something given
> And taken, in a lifetime's death in love,
> Ardour and selflessness and self-surrender.
> For most of us, there is only the unattended
> Moment, the moment in and out of time,

The distraction fit, lost in a shaft of sunlight,
The wild thyme unseen, or the winter lightning
Or the waterfall, or music heard so deeply
That it is not heard at all, but you are the music
While the music lasts. These are only hints and guesses,
Hints followed by guesses, and the rest
Is prayer, observance, discipline, thought, action.
The hint half guessed, the gift half understood is
    Incarnation.
Here the impossible union is actual,
Here the past and future
Are conquered, and reconciled.

Incarnation is the Logos of creation through whom all things are made. We, creatures fabricated of both matter and spirit, of aspects both visible and invisible, are, in Christ the Logos, the fulcrum of Incarnation.

Humbly loving and serving, choosing the other's good over our own immediate satisfactions, lifting our living to the Father in company with all the saints, we weave the "wedding garment" that is at once our theosis—admission to the feast of unending joy in the Father, Son, and Holy Spirit—and the Kingdom God is building with ourselves, the living stones.

The last hour before we retire for the night, Compline appears to share the darkness of Matins but, by now, Christ has so fully illumined the hours that even night

is light. Now we see the nothingness of dark, the evanes-
cence of evil. Compline is blinding luminosity in which
we not only see, but are aware of being seen.

> O Lord, You have searched me and known me!
> You know when I sit down and when I rise up;
> You penetrate my thoughts from afar.
> Whether I walk or lie down, You know it;
> All my paths are familiar to You.
> A word is hardly on my tongue
> Before You, O Lord, know it inside and out.
> You encompass me both behind and in front,
> Resting Your hand upon me.
> Such knowledge is too marvelous for me,
> So high I cannot attain it.
> Where can I flee from Your Spirit?
> Or where shall I hide from Your face?
> If I scale the heavens, You are there!
> If I descend to the world of the dead, You are there!
> If I fly with the wings of the dawn
> And dwell beyond the edge of the furthest seas,
> Even there Your hand shall guide me
> And Your right hand shall hold me fast.
> If I should say, "Surely darkness shall hide me;
> May the light about me be night,"
> Even darkness is not dark to You.
> The night illumines as the day,
> For to You darkness is as light.
> You formed my inward parts,

Knitting me together in my mother's womb.
Thank You! for I am wonderfully made,
Wonderful, as are all Your works;
My soul You knew very well;
My frame held no mysteries for You
Who were fashioning it in secret,
Skillfully shaping it in the depths of earth.
Your eyes saw my unformed substance;
In Your book were written, every one of them,
The days that were fixed for me
When they had not yet come to be.
(PSALM 139:1–16)

This, the brightest hour, is most truly the "cup that spills over." It captures and holds to overflowing the shining of the Sun, not the sun that set with the coming of evening, but the Sun who conquers death and darkness. The hour before we sleep, it can be a time of deepest prayer when we cast ourselves completely, confidently on the mercy of our Father with our final offering of the day. By the light of Compline, we review that day, holding it up to the scrutiny of One who knows every fiber of our inmost being.

But who is aware of all his errors?
From hidden evil cleanse me.
Preserve Your servant from arrogance, too,

That it may not have dominion over me!
Then I will be innocent of the great sin.
May the spoken words of my mouth
And the murmurings of my heart
Find favor before You, O Lord,
My rock, my redeemer!
(PSALM 19:13–15)

Not satisfied with conforming our actions and words to God, we lift the deepest recesses of our heart to Him so that His light may shine on them, burning away whatever is incompatible with His presence.

"May the spoken words of my mouth and the murmurings of my heart find favor before You, O Lord." The inclusion of the fifty-first psalm, thought to have been David's confession after sinning with Bathsheba, in both Sext and Compline services indicates a strong link between the two hours. For the deep peace of Compline rests securely on both the recognition of the truth of our sinful nature and its healing through the cross of Christ.

Penitence, far from requiring self-absorbed scrutiny of our every nook and cranny, is the result of "standing before God with our mind in our heart." The brighter the light in which we stand, the closer to its source, the more glaring our deficiencies appear. At times, such awareness may provoke tears, but they are only a prelude to joy.

Have mercy on me, O God, in Your great kindness.
According to the multitude of Your tender mercies,
Blot out my transgressions.
Scrub away my guilt, again and again,
And cleanse me from my fault.
For I know my transgressions
And my sin is always before me.
Against You, You alone, have I sinned,
Doing what is evil in Your sight.
Thus You may be found just when You pass sentence,
And blameless when You judge.
For behold, I was brought forth into iniquity;
Into sin, when my mother conceived me.
But Your delight is in interior truth;
In the secret depths of my heart You teach me wisdom.

Purge me with hyssop and I shall be cleansed;
Wash me and I shall be made whiter than snow.
Let me hear sounds of rejoicing and gladness,
That the bones You have broken may dance!
Turn Your face from my iniquities and blot out all my sin!
Create a clean heart in me, O God,
And renew a steadfast spirit within me.
Neither cast me from Your presence
Nor withdraw Your Holy Spirit from within me.
Restore to me the joy of Your healing
And sustain in me a generous spirit.
Then I will teach sinners Your ways,
Bringing back to You those who stray.
Absolve me from the guilt of bloodshed, O God,

And my tongue shall acclaim Your holiness;
O Lord, open my lips, and my mouth shall declare Your
    praise.
For in sacrifice You take no delight;
A burnt offering from me You would refuse.
Sacrifice to God is a bruised spirit;
A humbled and contrite heart, O God, You will not scorn.
May Your good will bring prosperity to Zion;
Build again the walls of Jerusalem.
Then lawful sacrifice will please You:
Burnt offerings and whole burnt offerings.
Then shall they offer young bulls on Your altar.
(PSALM 51)

The word "Compline" is from the Latin *completorium*, meaning the hour that completes the others. It is characterized by simplicity and wholeness, having evolved from the ancient practice of praying before falling asleep.

As a liturgical hour we first hear of it in the East from St. Basil in the middle of the fourth century. In the West, St. Benedict, influenced by Basil's rule, introduced it at the beginning of the sixth century into his own rule. While Western versions remain simple, the Eastern hour has been split into two parts, both somewhat elaborate.

Three psalms were prescribed by St. Benedict for Compline: Psalms 4, 91, and 134, all of which are among those used for Orthodox Complines. Both East and West intuit the essence of this hour, when darkness shrouds all but the lights that pierce it, choosing psalms that comfort. Our last acts of the day recall the immense and tender love of the One in whose presence we "live, move, and have our being."

> What is good has been made known to you, O man,
> And what the Lord requires of you:
> To fulfill justice, to love kindness,
> And to walk humbly with your God.
> (MICAH 6:8)

The final hour before a new creation awakens with Matins, Compline is a foretaste of the "peace surpassing all understanding" (Philippians 4:7). It wraps our strivings and work with contentment. There is no room here for agitation, for flight from God to the embrace of distractions vying to replace Him in our hearts. (And how often is "religion" one of them?)

Perhaps the most insidious form of flight from God, "religion" can clothe our darkness with the appearance of good. But Compline is incompatible with delusion. In that hour we are naked before God. Perhaps that is why prayers before sleep so often refer to death, the ultimate Compline, in which the presence of God will reveal what we have made of our hours and they, of us.

Simple as the breathing of a sleeping child, the prayer of Compline is the fullness of "standing before God with your mind in your heart," a translucent heart brimming with gratitude and joy. At this point we don't have to strain to see with God's eyes. His vision has become natural to us because we are living His life, animated by His Spirit.

We have viewed the hours as progression through both day and year without alluding to our personal seasons of youth, prime of life, and old age. The hours easily group themselves: Matins, Lauds, and Prime correspond to youth; Tierce, Sext, and Nones to maturity, with Vespers its culmination; and Compline, old age.

If one's point of view encompasses only what is experienced between birth and death, fear of death becomes the underlying motive for much of our activity. For what else are we fleeing when we race from addiction to addiction, when we plunge into ceaseless distractions or drown our spirits in frenetic activity? What do we seek to prove when we turn ourselves inside out to preserve ourselves as teenagers? As though immortality could be achieved by pickling adolescence!

A life of prayer, because it unites us to the source of true life, is the fountain of youth we mistakenly seek in the plastic surgeon's office. Aging is not a dread disease but the natural weaning of our bodies from materiality. It can be accompanied by the accumulated wisdom of a good life, great clarity, and the deepest joys we are able to experience in time.

The beauty of youth, while pleasing to the eye, has yet to undergo the sculpting that releases the spirit and allows one's inner light to reveal what God is creating. Compline, like the other hours, should be joyfully embraced. We are closer to both our beginning and our end.

Sleep, the letting go of our hold on the day through which we have just passed, is a metaphor for death, the relinquishing of all our hours. If, as with the seed, our end is implicit in our beginning, it is also true that our beginning only makes complete sense in our "end," when we die. The meaning of our hours is who we have become in the moment of distillation, when all that is temporal leaves us to our essence and we pass from this world to the next.

Dwelling on imaginary details of the life to come, describing the furniture of an existence we cannot comprehend, is an exercise in futility that has tempted far too many Christian preachers over the centuries. Their Master did not indulge in it.

Within the parenthesis between life and death we are able to act and to know. It is there, in our "hours," that we may "be strengthened with might through His Spirit in the inner man, that Christ may dwell in [our] hearts through faith; that [we], being rooted and grounded in love, may be able to comprehend with all the saints what is the width and length and depth and height—to know the love of Christ which surpasses knowledge, that [we] may be filled with all the fullness of God" (Ephesians 3:16–19).

One completely "filled with all the fullness of God," Mary the Mother of God, is especially remembered in our evening and night prayers. Scripture says little of her, allowing its silence to mimic hers, inscribing her image with a few graceful lines. She, by the Holy Spirit, incarnated her Son in female form.

If we know Him, we know her, for the wisdom of the People of God has always known the two are inseparable. The close embrace of Christ and the Church is imaged in the embrace of mother and Son. For she did not just give birth to Him as a separate human being; she also gave birth to Him in her heart, as we are called to do.

That is the meaning of Christ's words when He answered the woman who cried, "Happy is the womb that bore You and the breasts that nursed You!" In reply He said, "They are happier who hear the word of God and observe it" (Luke 11:27–28). No action of ours, no honor, can be a greater blessing than aligning ourselves with God as she did when she said, "Be it done unto me according to Your word" (Luke 1:38).

Luke, the evangelist who tells us most about Mary, includes her Magnificat in his first chapter, where he records the great events that changed, not only her life, but that of the whole world. Mary's is the voice of Israel, the grateful servant of the Lord, but her prayer, while echoing themes in Hannah's hymn from 1 Samuel 2, is more personal, as though in her being she summed up and transcended the tradition of Israel.

> My life celebrates the Lord, and my spirit rejoices in
> God my Savior,
> Because He has allowed His glance to fall upon His
> lowly handmaiden.
> From this day forth all generations will call me blessed
> Because He-Who-Is-Mighty has raised me up.
> Holy is His name, and His mercy extends from
> generation to generation
> To those who fear Him.
> He has shown the power of His arm,
> Scattering the proud in the conceit of their hearts.
> He has cast down the powerful and lifted up the lowly,
> Filling the hungry with good things and sending the
> rich away empty.
> He has accepted Israel, His servant mindful of His mercy,

As He promised our fathers: to Abraham and his seed
for all ages.

As we are about to close our eyes in sleep, Holy
Mother Church presents us with an icon of the Theotokos: the "orans." In it Mary becomes the image of prayer
with her hands raised, the image of silent supplication,
of the divinized human person lifting the world in praise
and gratitude to the Father through the Son in the Holy
Spirit.

Mary the mother of Jesus is not only the culmination
of Israelite tradition; she is the best humanity has to offer.
Perhaps we may learn from her obscurity and her silence.
She, the antithesis of worldly achievement, of "assertive-
ness," is quietly confident. We see it in her *fiat* and in the
calm directive to the servants at the wedding feast of Cana:
"Do as He tells you," uttered despite her Son's apparent
disinclination to draw attention to Himself at that time.

Becoming prayer is becoming whole. Compline celebrates that wholeness, the time when the process of inte-
grating our fragments is achieved. Adam was not complete in himself, but needed Eve, because human nature
is both masculine and feminine. In Compline, as well as
in the cycle of major feasts, the Church recognizes this
truth, carefully balancing her presentation of the life of

Christ with that of His mother so that the masculine does not overbalance the feminine.

In the Eastern Church calendar, which runs from September to August, the major feasts begin with Mary's birth and end with her death. So, too, in the Divine Liturgy, from time to time remembrance of the Theotokos breaks into the celebration so that we never lose sight of the whole, of the feminine, despite the predominance of the male in the events we represent.

"Precious in the sight of the Lord is the death of His saints" and peaceful (Psalm 116:15). For the saints live a foretaste of heaven in this life. They need no one else to describe the future toward which they are traveling because the Kingdom of Heaven is already within them and near them. Like candle flames of love, they radiate concentric circles of light wherever they are and, like spiders, they spin from within a web of love strong enough to snare the willing with its delicate beauty.

> When the Lord restored the fortunes of Zion,
> We were like those who dream.
> Then our mouth was filled with laughter,
> And our tongue with shouts of joy;
> Then they said among the nations,
> "The Lord has done great things for them."
> The Lord has done great things for us, and we are glad.

Restore our fortunes, O Lord,
Like streams in the Negeb!
Those who sow in tears shall reap with shouts of joy!
He who goes out weeping, bearing the seed for
    sowing,
Shall return with shouts of joy, carrying his sheaves
    with him.
(PSALM 126)

Making the sign of the cross as we pray the ancient Trisagion, "Holy God, Holy Mighty, Holy Immortal, have mercy on us" (*Agios o Theos, Agios Ischyros, Agios Athanatos, eleison imas*), we bow deeply toward the icons, where Vesper candles have been snuffed. We no longer need them. The moon and stars, lit by the hands of our Father, are light enough for eyes illumined from within.

The psalms, which we have threaded through the hours in recognition of the Church's practice (following ancient Jewish custom), end in a burst of pure praise. The Holy Spirit, who inspired not only the composers but also the collectors and arrangers of the psalms, moves the Psalter from Psalm 1, describing the holy man, through many modes and moods to purest prayer, mimicking the development of the pray-er. Void of self, the last psalms are so rapt in love and contemplation of God that they seem to soar off the page.

Praise the Lord!
Praise the Lord from the heavens;
Praise Him from the heights!
Praise Him, all His angels;
Praise Him, all His hosts!
Praise Him, sun and moon,
Praise Him, all you shining stars!
Praise Him, you highest heavens,
And you waters above the heavens!
Let them praise the name of the Lord!
For He commanded and they were created,
And He established them forever and ever;
For He gave a decree, and it shall not pass away.
Praise the Lord from the earth,
You great sea creatures and all deeps,
Fire and hail, snow and mist,
Stormy wind fulfilling His word!
Mountains and all hills,
Fruit trees and all cedars!
Beasts and all livestock,
Creeping things and flying birds!
Kings of the earth and all peoples,
Princes and rulers of the earth!
Young men and maidens together,
Old men and children!
Let them praise the name of the Lord,
For His name alone is exalted;
His majesty is above earth and heaven.
He has raised up a horn for His people,
Praise for all His saints,

For the people of Israel who are near to Him.
Praise the Lord!
(PSALM 148)

Our final miniature? The frame is a night sky, blackness pierced by stars. They seem fixed only if one does not contemplate them over time. If in stillness we are attentive, we not only perceive movement, we hear an unearthly music. It invites us beyond the frame into the picture itself, which appears blank but, once we are within it, assumes familiar shapes. By the light of a rising moon we can make out the place we have come to, but because "here" is different for each of us, I cannot describe it.

But you will recognize your living space, its rooms, its faces, the trees that shelter it or the tall buildings standing outside. Owls may hoot in its woods or seagulls cry and swoop above its streets. You may see your front door opening into your home or out onto the familiar world that surrounds it. If it is Compline, you will see it with a purified heart.

The image has been shaped by your response to what God has placed before you, what you have chosen to do and how you have chosen to respond.

You have chosen its furnishings, the little mementos of your journey and of those you have loved. There may be toys on the floor, papers on your desk, tools in the cellar, a laundry basket piled high with clothes. The table has been surrounded by your family and friends; windows frame living pictures, pieces of the larger world beyond your shaping.

Through this miniature you enter the Kingdom of heaven—or not at all.

If we are prayer, love has shaped the place in which we find ourselves at the end of the day. Our pots have held love in the shape of food; our chairs have cushioned the bodies of those we honor with our home; our windows open onto scenes depicting love, either present or apparently absent.

Compline penetrates to the truth that Love is never really absent. Even when humans deny or reject Him, Love is present, pressing in upon us without injuring our freedom to refuse Him if we choose.

In peace let us pray to the Lord.

Notes

1   Quotations from Scripture are my own translations, using four English versions (Ronald Knox's translation, the *English Standard Version*, the post-Vatican II revised *Liturgy of the Hours*, and the Oxford *Jerusalem Bible)*, the Latin Vulgate, and the Greek New Testament, with prayer to the Holy Spirit. The effort was to make the English as understandable and graceful as I knew how.

2   Advent is the first season of the church year, beginning in mid-November for the Orthodox and on the fourth Sunday before December 25 for the Western Church. It is a period of anticipation before the Feast of the Nativity of Christ, analogous to the forty days of Lent before Easter. Affinity for darkness and Israel's long preparation for the Messiah are themes expressed in Advent liturgies, which tend to have a gentle, meditative quality, reminiscent of Mary's gestation of the Word and the way she kept things in her heart, pondering them.

3   My use of the word *tenebrae* here is allusive. It has come to mean shadowy darkness with overtones of mystery and an emphasis on the shadows. But it also carries referential meanings derived from both the Latin and services called by the same name. The Latin meanings include darkness, night, blindness, ignorance, obscurity, gloom, a dark place, prison.

        Tenebrae were also pre-Vatican II Holy Week services conducted on the evenings before Holy Thursday, Holy Friday, and Holy Saturday to express the dark side of Christ's suffering and our bereavement, so that *tenebrae* has the sense of the dark world without Christ.

Some see in these services a reflection of the Jewish customs connected with the fast day of Tisha B'Av, which commemorates the destruction of Solomon's temple in 586 BC; Roman demolition of the rebuilt temple in AD 70; the expulsion of Jews from England in 1290 and from Spain in 1492; the beginning of WWII and the Holocaust.

4   The quotation from St. Theophan the Recluse is found on p. 17 of *The Art of Prayer: An Orthodox Anthology* (London: Faber & Faber, 1997). His thoughts are amplified with those of other saintly monks in this truly helpful and profound collection compiled by Igumen Chariton of Valamo and translated by E. Kadloubovsky and E. M. Palmer, with an introduction by Timothy Ware (Bishop Kallistos of Diocleia).

5   H. V. Morton, *In the Steps of the Master* (Cambridge, MA: Da Capo Press, 2002), p. 3. This book, by one of the best travel writers ever, was written before Israel became a nation. It has the merit of preserving for us a Palestine very like the one in which Christ lived. Morton brings to his considerable skills as an observer and writer his profound faith and the sort of intellectual background capable of exploring this land as no one else could.

6   R .L. Wilken, *The Spirit of Early Christian Thought: Seeking the Face of God* (New Haven: Yale University Press, 2003, pp. 40–41). This is an excellent book for anyone wishing to explore the thinking of the early Fathers of the Church in their context. While the book yields most fruit if one has a background in patristics, there is an abundance for anyone wishing to explore the topic.

7   For an in-depth treatment of baptism, see Alexander Schmemann, *Of Water and the Spirit* (Crestwood, NY: St. Vladimir's Seminary Press, 2004), and Kilian McDonnell, *The Baptism of Jesus in the Jordan* (Collegeville, MN: Michael Glazier Books, 1996).

8   This is the Orthodox view: that we're born into a world distorted by sin. The Western position is that we have inherited a stain on our souls that is transmitted from parents to children and that we are incapable of any good without the grace of God. The West sees a more thorough and complete Fall while the East's view, more optimistic, less deterministic, is of a partial Fall with no inherited sin.

9   Neither Emilie Van Taack nor I have been able to pin down her quotation. I believe it is from a lecture she gave.

10 *Theosis* is the Greek word used in Orthodoxy to refer to the transformation which occurs in a Christian who is responsive to the Holy Spirit. It follows *metanoia* and is best exemplifed by Mary, the Mother of God, and by the saints.

11 St. Isaac of Nineveh's quotations may be found in Bishop Kallistos Ware's *The Orthodox Way* (Crestwood, NY: St. Vladimir's Seminary Press, 1995) on pages 114, 55, and 133. There are collections of St. Isaac's writings in English, but the state of scholarship regarding them is so far from settled that it would probably be wiser to wait for a critical edition. *The Orthodox Way* is a wonderfully rich, allusive presentation of Christianity accessible to anyone desiring deeper understanding of the Christian tradition or an Eastern Christian approach to it.

12 Although some have attributed the Akathist to Father Gregory, it was actually written by Metropolitan Tryphon (Prince Boris Petrovich Turkestanov), who died in 1934.

13 The *Shema Y'israel* is the prime affirmation and fundamental prayer of Judaism. Its most essential part is, "Hear, O Israel, the Lord is our God; the only God" (Deuteronomy 6:4). It is followed by, "You shall love the Lord your God with all your heart and with all your soul and with all your strength. May these words that I command you today remain in your heart. You shall teach them diligently to your sons and shall speak of them when you sit in your house, as well as when you walk along the road, and when you lie down and when you rise. You shall bind them as a sign

on your hand, and on your forehead, like a headband. You shall write them on the doorposts of your house and on your gates" (Deuteronomy 6:7–9).

The *Shema* is recited by devout Jews morning and evening, and on their deathbed. In Jewish liturgy, it also includes Deuteronomy 11:13–21 and Numbers 15:37–41.

14   Henri J. M. Nouwen, *Behold the Beauty of the Lord: Praying with Icons* (Notre Dame: Ave Maria Press, 1996), p. 14. This is a lovely little book for Westerners hoping for insight into icons. Another is Archbishop Rowan Williams' *Ponder These Things* (Brewster, MA: Paraclete Press, 2006).

15   Pavel Florensky, *Iconostasis*, translated by Donald Sheehan and Olga Andrejev (Crestwood, NY: St. Vladimir's Seminary Press, 1996), p. 65. This wonderful book is not for everyone, but will reward those who are up to it with profound insight.

16   *The Treasures of the Monastery of St. Catherine of Sinai* (foreword by Archbishop Damianos of Sinai; photos: Araldo de Luca; text: Corinna Rossi; Vercelli, Italy: White Star Publishers, 2006) is not only a stunningly beautiful book but an evocative presentation of a place of profound revelation for both Jews and Christians. The burning bush; the Israelite sojourn in the desert with its images of manna, cloud, pillar of fire; and the Ten Commandments hallowed the Sinai long before Christianity.

This starkly beautiful desert landscape gave birth to the first monastic communities, and on this spot a monastery has stood since the fourth century, when St. Helen ordered one built. That her orders were carried out is corroborated by Egeria, a Spanish woman who visited there in 384 and who describes what she encountered in a long letter to her friends.

Until recently, this holy place tended to be overlooked by the West, despite its intimate connections with early monasticism and with St. John Climacus, St. Helen, and St. Catherine, to say nothing of its seminal relationship to the events of the Old Testament, its icons, and its manuscript collection, second only to those of the Vatican.

17 Florensky, *Iconostasis,* pp. 61–62.

18 The icon of St. Genevieve and several others from the hand of the master iconographer, Gregory Kroug, a Russian émigré monk living in Paris, are beautifully reproduced in an oversized book by Father Andrew Tregubov: *The Light of Christ* (Crestwood, NY: St. Vladimir's Seminary Press, 1990). Icons and commentary combine to offer one an encounter not possible in a smaller book.

19 The basic facts of St. Jacob's life are easily accessible through Wikipedia or Orthodoxwiki online.

20 Two good expositions of the Jesus Prayer are *The Way of the Pilgrim* by an anonymous nineteenth-century Russian (Boston, 1991) and Per-Olof Sjogren, Dean of Gothenburg Cathedral's *The Jesus Prayer* (London: Society for Promoting Christian Knowledge, 1996).

21 Quoted in *The Orthodox Way*, p. 130.

22 *The Syriac Fathers on Prayer and the Spiritual Life,* translated and with an introduction by Sebastian Brock (Kalamazoo, MI: Cistercian Publications, 1987), p. 67. This book is a treasure of luminous spiritual insight into prayer from those great practitioners of it in what are now Syria, Iraq, Iran, Qutar, and environs.

23 Father Alexander Schmemann's *For the Life of the World* (Crestwood, NY: St. Vladimir's Seminary Press, 2004, p. 23) was the catalyst for my own understanding of the world's dying when it rejected Christ. Anyone interested in deepening understanding of the sacraments would do well to read the whole book.

24 For a profound exploration of eucharistic ecclesiology see John D. Zizioulas, *Being as Communion: Studies in Personhood and the Church* (Crestwood, NY: St. Vladimir's Seminary Press, 2002). It is not for everyone. But those whose theological and philosophical backgrounds can support it will find its extraordinary insights well worth digesting.

25   There are many editions of St. Augustine's *Confessions,* but it is also easily accessible online as *The Confessions of St. Augustine: An Electronic Edition,* James J. O'Donnell, 1992, or as a free e-book at <http://www.gutenberg.org/etext/3296>. Chapter X, "On Memory," is a thought-provoking exploration of the topic.

26   Schmemann, *For the Life of the World,* p. 14.

27   The story is from an article by Father Peter Knowles, O.P.: "Eastern Monasticism—Symbol and Synthesis of Christianity." <http://www.catholicukes.org.au/tiki-download_file.php? fileId=680>

28   "Greek Orthodox" is found on p. 319 of *John Betjeman: Collected Poems* (New York, John Murray Publishers, Ltd., 2006).

29   H. V. Morton, *In the Steps of the Master,* p. 184.

Christ in the Psalms
by Patrick Henry Reardon

A highly inspirational book of meditations on the Psalms by one of the most insightful and challenging Orthodox writers of our day. Avoiding both syrupy sentimentality and arid scholasticism, *Christ in the Psalms* takes the reader on a thought-provoking and enlightening pilgrim-age through this beloved "prayer book" of the Church. Which psalms were quoted most frequently in the New Testament, and how were they interpreted? How has the Church historically understood and utilized the various psalms in her liturgical life? How can we perceive the image of Christ shining through the Psalms? Lively and highly devotional, thought-provoking yet warm and practical, *Christ in the Psalms* sheds a world of insight upon each psalm, and offers practical advice for how to make the Psalter a part of our daily lives.

• Paperback, 328 pages (ISBN: 978-1-888212-21-1) CP No. 004927—$17.95*

Bread & Water, Wine & Oil
An Orthodox Christian Experience of God
by Fr. Meletios Webber

Worry, despair, insecurity, fear of death . . . these are our daily com-panions. It is precisely where we hurt most that the experience of the Orthodox Church has much to offer. The remedy is not any simple admonitions to fight the good fight, cheer up, or think positively. Rather, the Orthodox method is to change the way we look at the human person (starting with ourselves). Orthodoxy shows us how to "be transformed by the renewing of our mind"—a process that is aided by participation in the traditional ascetic practices and Mysteries of the Church. In this unique and accessible book, Archimandrite Meletios Webber first explores the role of mystery in the Christian life, then walks the reader through the seven major Mysteries (or sacraments) of the Orthodox Church, showing the way to a richer, fuller life in Christ.

• Paperback, 200 pages (ISBN: 978-1-888212-91-4) CP No. 006324—$15.95*

Seasons of Grace
Reflections on the Church Year
by Donna Farley

We sometimes find ourselves walking a tightrope between what we think is the ideal of a holy life and the demands of our postmodern world. The

beauty of the Church seasons is that they teach us how to balance our life. This collection is author Donna Farley's own view from the tightrope. These short yet thoughtful reflections, written in an insightful and sometimes humorous style, will help weave together the great feasts into the fabric of our lives.
• Paperback, 195 pages (ISBN: 978-1-888212-50-1) CP No. 005658—$14.95*

Let Us Attend
A Journey Through the Orthodox Divine Liturgy
by Father Lawrence Farley
Esteemed author and Scripture commentator Fr. Lawrence Farley provides a guide to understanding the Divine Liturgy, and a vibrant reminder of the centrality of the Eucharist in living the Christian life.

Every Sunday morning we are literally taken on a journey into the Kingdom of God. Fr. Lawrence guides believers in a devotional and historical walk through the Orthodox Liturgy. Examining the Liturgy section by section, he provides both historical explanations of how the Liturgy evolved and devotional insights aimed at helping us pray the Liturgy in the way the Fathers intended. In better understanding the depth of the Liturgy's meaning and purpose, we can pray it properly. If you would like a deeper understanding of your Sunday morning experience so that you can draw closer to God, then this book is for you.
• Paperback, 104 pages (ISBN: 978-1-888212-87-7) CP No. 007295—$10.95*

Mary, Worthy of Praise
Reflections on the Virgin Mary
by Fr. David Smith
The Paraklesis service offers the perfect vehicle for us to consider the place of Mary in our lives. Fr. David Smith shares with us his own personal meditations on Mary, based upon his reflections on the Paraklesis service.
• Paperback, 118 pages (ISBN: 978-1-888212-71-6) CP No. 006599—$11.95*

*Plus applicable tax and postage & handling charges. Prices current as of 8/2010. Please call Conciliar Press at 800-967-7377 for complete ordering information, or order online at www.conciliarpress.com.

 **ANCIENT FAITH RADIO**
Visit www.ancientfaithradio.com to listen to podcasts of interest.